HOUGHTON LIBRARY AT 75

HOUGHTON LIBRARY AT 75

A CELEBRATION OF ITS COLLECTIONS

HOUGHTON LIBRARY
HARVARD UNIVERSITY

DISTRIBUTED BY HARVARD UNIVERSITY PRESS
CAMBRIDGE, MASSACHUSETTS • LONDON, ENGLAND

2017

FRONTISPIECE:

Laurent de Brunhoff (1925–). *Babar brings his ABC to Houghton Library,* **2016.**
TypDr 2070.B240.16b. Watercolor, gouache, graphite and ink on Arches
watercolor paper. 11 by 11½ in. Commissioned by Houghton Library to celebrate
the acquisition of the complete archive of preparatory materials for Jean de
Brunhoff's *ABC de Babar.*

Logo design by Susan Wyssen, 2016.

ISBN 978-0-674-98008-2

FOREWORD

Houghton Library opened its doors on February 28, 1942, stirring public interest and no shortage of coverage in the nation's newspapers. A "collection-de-luxe in a building elegantly ornate" according to a *Boston Globe* editorial, it boasted modern amenities such as climate control and fluorescent lighting, and was hailed in the *New York Times* as nothing less than a "bookman's dream." It was, however, something more. The entry of the United States into the Second World War just two months prior elevated an occasion of note, as a writer in the *New York Herald Tribune* wrote, to "an act of faith" and "an affirmation of the importance of cultural studies" at a moment when civilization appeared to be unraveling. An impulse to preserve and understand "the vital records of human aspiration and growth," long the province of libraries, was heightened by circumstance and enshrined in a space that exalted the pursuit of knowledge.

Seventy-five years later, we celebrate an institution that continues to affirm the value of dogged inquiry and joyful discovery, shining a light on humanity's ambitions and achievements across time and space. The following pages offer a glimpse not just of the Houghton Library's extraordinary collections, but also of the remarkable variety of human creativity and effort that wrought them. Through a fragment of Homer's *Odyssey*, Phillis Wheatley's poetry, and Ralph Waldo Emerson's journal, we enter into conversation with people of another era—both those who create and those who preserve—to see and understand different worlds and to look with new eyes on the present. We encounter names familiar and unfamiliar, imagine authors anonymous or lost to time, and reflect

Construction on Houghton
Harvard University Arc'

TOM HYRY
Florence Fearrington Librarian of Houghton Library
of the Harvard College Library
HOUGHTON LIBRARY
HARVARD UNIVERSITY · CAMBRIDGE · MASSACHUSETTS 02138
T 617-495-2441
F 617-495-1376
E hcl@fas.harvard.edu
W hcl.harvard.edu/houghton

on words and ideas that have relevance for our contemporary lives.

Many of the rare or unique materials in our collections have been digitized, and people around the world can now explore, learn, and question without ever traveling to Cambridge, a significant change that has influenced how we think about libraries and their roles in intellectual life. Yet we should be reluctant to let newfound convenience overshadow time-honored experience. Artifacts are the physical and material embodiment of a past that still shapes us, and they create a bridge between what was and what is—and invite us to cross it by virtue of their very existence. Is anything as exhilarating as encountering the thing itself?

The world has changed rapidly in the three-quarters of a century since Houghton Library took its place among the nation's great university libraries, but it has remained the same in important ways as well. Individuals continue to give generously to enlarge our collections, and our librarians continue to ensure that extraordinarily diverse materials enrich scholarship and teaching at Harvard and elsewhere. Perhaps most importantly, rare book and manuscript libraries remain sacred spaces. In their cool and quiet confines, one discovers the possibility of transcendence, of seeking and understanding mingled with lasting faith in humanity and all it has created.

Drew Gilpin Faust

President of Harvard University
and Lincoln Professor of History

Laura Wulf. *Houghton Library with tulips*, 1989. Harvard University Archives, HUV 49.2, Box 3, folder 6.

As it was seventy-five years ago, rare book and manuscript libraries today remain defined by the quality and the scale of their collections. But as we take great and justifiable pride in Houghton's collections, we remember and assert that libraries are not mere assemblages but instead inherently social entities, constructed in all ways through the judgment, dedication, and inspiration of librarians, scholars, students, collectors, donors, and others whose lives and activities intersect with the library.

Were Houghton merely the sum of the parts of its collection, there would be little to celebrate. Houghton's books and manuscripts brim with potential energy and we take pride not only in the knowledge held and preserved in the library, but especially in the new discoveries and creations we enable and inspire. So in celebrating the collection, we must also appreciate the work and insight of the founders of the library and our many colleagues past and present who have worked with great passion and purpose not only to acquire and preserve these materials but also to connect them to writers, artists, students, and many others asking questions and seeking truths found only at Houghton. And in that context, I want to congratulate Heather Cole and John Overholt for the masterful job they have done in choosing for this book a representative sample of texts and artifacts to demonstrate the remarkable depth and breadth of Houghton collections.

As we continue to build upon the legacy of Houghton's collections, two significant challenges stand out. Houghton now seeks to actively welcome a broader community into the library, becoming less of a bastion for the privileged. We must continue, likewise, to broaden our collecting mandate to include materials that document a more diverse representation of humanity. Additionally, the remarkable transformations wrought by new information technologies that have emerged over the past generation provide a myriad of challenges and opportunities. As the record of contemporary society and culture becomes increasingly complex and largely created on digital media, Houghton's collections will evolve accordingly. By Houghton's sesquicentennial, a spectacular collection of digital materials will accompany and complement the physical texts and artifacts that largely comprise the library today.

It would be foolish to presume that the next seventy-five years will see any less change than we have experienced since the library opened its doors. We can, however, expect Houghton to remain a leading center for preserving and sharing knowledge in order to help society understand and learn from its best and worst moments, spread awareness of a diverse set of cultures, educate new generations of citizens and leaders, and foster understanding of the past in order to navigate a complex present and construct a better future. This noble mission endures.

THOMAS HYRY

Florence Fearrington Librarian of Houghton Library and Director of Arts and Special Collections of the Harvard College Library

Exhibition Room, 1942. MS Stor 322.

INTRODUCTION

In the summer of 1924, Archibald Cary Coolidge, Director of the Harvard University Library, outlined his initial vision of what would become Houghton Library in a letter to his colleague George Parker Winship: "What I do dream of is a beautiful building . . . in which we store all our works of great rarity and value . . . [and] works dear to the book-lover, a place where we could keep what we valued most and show it to those who appreciate it . . . We might put this enchanted palace on the raised ground close to Widener . . ." (Coolidge to Winship, June 25, 1924, reproduced in Kenneth E. Carpenter, "A note on the origins of the Houghton Library," *Harvard Library Bulletin* 5, no. 3 (1994): 4). In 1940, this plan took concrete shape as Harvard librarians William A. Jackson and Philip Hofer met with Arthur A. Houghton Jr., who sketched out a design for the library that would open bearing his name in 1942, thanks to a gift of stock in his family's company, Corning Glass Works.

Seventy-five years later, Arthur Houghton would find much about the library familiar from his sketch, but the way in which it operates has been dramatically transformed. Houghton Library was born into a world still ruled largely by paper—not just in its collections, but in the systems by which those collections were managed. Researchers consulted card catalogs and filled out paper slips to request the materials they wanted to see. Those who could not visit in person sent letters of inquiry, and reference librarians responded with typewritten replies, with a carbon copy kept for the library files.

The Houghton of 2017 is as digital as the world around it. Researchers consult online catalogs and submit electronic requests at the touch of a button.

Each day, staff field emailed questions by the dozens. Our digitized collections (at least those free of copyright restrictions) are as accessible in Kyoto as in Cambridge, and have dramatically expanded the communities we serve. Though the vast majority of our holdings still consist of works on paper, as we continue to collect the work of contemporary authors we are increasingly grappling with the challenges of preserving and making accessible the panoply of digital storage formats that have arisen since the birth of personal computing.

Despite vastly different methods of searching for collections and communicating with those who use them, Houghton's first curators would most likely still recognize in our collecting the foundational concentrations established with the library's first acquisitions.

Houghton serves as the primary special collections repository to support Harvard College and the Faculty of Arts and Sciences, and its collections represent the scope of human experience from ancient Egypt to twenty-first century Cambridge. With strengths primarily in North American and European history, literature, and culture, collections range in media from printed books and handwritten manuscripts to maps, drawings and paintings, prints, posters, photographs, film and audio recordings, and digital media, as well as costumes, theater props, and a wide range of other objects.

Materials are acquired through hundreds of distinct endowment funds, administered by curators in eight departments. In the past twenty-five years, the number of curatorial departments has expanded: along with the Printing and Graphic Arts department, the Harvard Theatre Collection, and the Theodore Roosevelt Collection, all incorporated into the library in its first two years, and the Harry Elkins Widener Collection, administered at Houghton

Houghton under construction, 1941. MS Stor 322.

Sidney Ives, from 1966–1980 Houghton's acquisitions bibliographer, on the Houghton bridge, which connected Widener Library to the Houghton reading room and contained Houghton's card catalogs. The bridge was demolished in 2004. MS Stor 322.

since 1969, the library now encompasses the Early Books and Manuscripts, the Donald and Mary Hyde Collection of Dr. Samuel Johnson and Early Modern Books and Manuscripts, and the Modern Books and Manuscripts departments, as well as the Woodberry Poetry Room in Lamont Library.

New acquisitions reflect not only the traditional collecting strengths of the library but also trends in scholarship and the varied ways researchers use our materials. The increasingly interdisciplinary nature of research and teaching presents new challenges and opportunities for collection building; the shift in the humanities towards uncovering suppressed or underrepresented voices has also significantly changed how curators approach acquisitions. We now recognize that our collecting must move beyond the privileged, white, male voices that traditionally dominated Houghton's shelves, and that recognition has broadened the scope of our new acquisitions, and led to a new focus on finding the underrepresented individuals and groups in our older collections.

In addition, acquisitions are increasingly driven by teaching and classroom use. In the past five years, class sessions (mainly for Harvard undergraduates but also for groups from a large number of colleges and universities across Massachusetts) have grown exponentially, and collection material is regularly incorporated into class assignments. Undergraduate use of collections in the reading room has also increased significantly, due to expanded outreach and new programs focusing on student research.

In setting out to capture the full diversity and impact of Houghton's collections in seventy-five snapshots, we have knowingly set ourselves an impossible task. No library this large and complex can be perfectly reduced to a book this size. Of necessity, we are only scratching the surface of a collection that represents some of the most precious items accumulated in the nearly 400-year history of the world's largest university library system.

That being said, we do hope that the items depicted here will serve as a useful introduction to Houghton and its mission of collecting artifacts of human thought and experience for the benefit of scholarly research and teaching. The book is arranged in chronological order, to suggest one important dimension of the collection: Houghton's holdings span nearly the whole history of the written word, from papyrus to the laptop. The objects range in size from miniature books composed by Charlotte Brontë to a massive gradual, a liturgical manuscript with text large enough for a choir to sing from. They celebrate great achievements in many different fields of human endeavor, from the plays of Shakespeare to the discoveries of Copernicus; from the photography of Angus McBean to the poetry of Emily Dickinson. Some items were acquired by Harvard long before Houghton was built, a few just before this book went to print.

Most importantly, each item is merely a particularly noteworthy representative of collections that run substantially deeper. Research thrives in collections that include not just the high water marks of history but also their context. Great creators stand out, but they cannot be fully understood without seeing their network of friends, families, and collaborators; the works they read; the full record of the lives they lived. Houghton seeks to provide scholars with these raw materials from which new knowledge is forged.

HEATHER COLE, *Assistant Curator of Modern Books & Manuscripts and Curator of the Theodore Roosevelt Collection*

JOHN OVERHOLT, *Curator of the Donald and Mary Hyde Collection of Dr. Samuel Johnson and Early Modern Books & Manuscripts*

January 2017

HOMER. FRAGMENT OF THE *ODYSSEY* ON PAPYRUS, CA. 1–200 CE.

Papyrus was a revolutionary communication technology and enjoyed a remarkably long period of use; the earliest surviving papyri date to the third millennium BCE in Egypt, and official papal decrees were still being issued on papyrus as late as 1000 CE. The deterioration of this piece makes it easier to see the method by which papyrus was made, laying strips of the plant first horizontally, then a second layer vertically. These lines of the *Odyssey* were copied, possibly as a student exercise, some one thousand years after their composition.

MS Gr SM2224.
7½ by 3½ in.
Deposited by the Harvard Semitic Museum,
ca. 1959.

THE EMERSON-WHITE HOURS, CA. 1480.

A book of hours is a small devotional work containing a liturgical calendar, and prayers and readings to be recited at particular times of the day. The Emerson-White Hours, so named for the modern owners of the manuscript, is an especially beautiful example of the form. Produced in Bruges in the late 15th century, this manuscript would likely have been specially commissioned by a member of a wealthy and noble family for use in a private chapel. Sadly, manuscripts as spectacular as this one were often picked apart by collectors and booksellers over the centuries, and today it lacks as many as 40 full-page illustrations it would once have contained.

MS Typ 443/MS Typ 443.1,
f. 102v (this page) and f. 62r.
Manuscript on vellum.
6 by 9 in. (when open).
Given in memory of William A. White and his daughter Frances White Emerson by members of their family: Harold White, Donald Moffat, and Mrs. John Wing, 1958.

Gradual, ca. 1515.

In sharp contrast to the pocket-sized book of hours shown on the preceding pages, this manuscript stands two feet high and is designed for communal rather than private worship; a gradual is a choir book large enough for a group to sing from at once. Houghton's volume is one of a set of four created in Rouen, France, in the early 16th century, with the remaining volumes now held at two libraries in the U.S. and one in Germany.

At his death in 1951, William King Richardson left Houghton an exquisite collection of some 1,700 books and manuscripts, not including those he had earlier donated to the library, such as this one. Richardson's generosity also provided the elegant room that had been awaiting them since the opening of the library. They remain there today as a testament to Richardson's exceptional eye for works of great beauty and importance.

MS Lat 186, f. 44v (this page) and f. 136r.
Manuscript on vellum.
29½ by 40 in. (when open).
Gift of William King Richardson, 1947.

Ilem

sti iusti

ciam et odisti ini

quita tem proptcrea

vn rit te de us

More than five and a half centuries after the Western invention of movable-type printing in Mainz, Germany, the Gutenberg Bible remains an object not just of veneration and inspiration, but, just as important in a university library, of study as well. Advances in digital imaging and analysis in recent years have added to our understanding of just how the book was produced. Harvard's copy, one of about 20 complete copies that survive today, is kept on permanent display in the Harry Elkins Widener Memorial Room in Widener Library, in tribute to the collector and Harvard alumnus who perished on the Titanic at the age of 27.

HEW Room, f. 5r (this page)
and f. 305r.
15½ by 25 in. (when open).
Gift of George D. Widener and
Eleanor Widener Dixon, 1944.

eos i terra. In fine ne disperdas dauid
i tituli inscriptoe qn misit saul et
custodiut domu eu ut interficeret eu
Eripe me de inimicis meis deus
meus: et ab insurgentibus in me
libera me. Eripe me de operantibus
iniquitatem: et de viris sanguinum
salua me. Quia ecce ceperunt anima
meam: irruerunt in me fortes. Neq;
iniquitas mea neq; peccatum meum
domine: sine iniquitate cucurri et di-
rexi. Exurge in occursum meum et
vide: et tu domine deus virtutum deus israhel. Intende ad visitandas
omnes gentes: non miserearis omni-
bus gentibus qui operantur iniquitatem. Conuertentur ad vesperam
et famem patientur ut canes: et circu-
ibunt ciuitatem. Ecce loquentur in
ore suo: et gladius in labijs eorum:
quoniam quis audiuit? Et tu domine deridebis eos: ad nichilum de-
duces omnes gentes. Fortitudine
meam ad te custodiam: quia deus susceptor meus: deus meus misericordia eius preueniet me. Deus ostendisti michi super inimicos meos: ne oc-
cidas eos nequando obliuiscantur
populi mei. Disperge illos i virtute
tua: et depone eos protector meus domine. Delictum oris eorum: sermo-
nem labiorum ipsorum: et compre-
hendantur in superbia sua. Et de
execratione et mendacio annuncia-
buntur in consummatione: in ira con-
summationis et non erunt. Et scient
quia deus dominabitur iacob: et fi-
nium terre. Conuertentur ad vesperam et famem patientur ut canes: et
circuibut ciuitatem. Ipsi dispergen-
tur ad manducandum: si vero non
fuerint saturati et murmurabut. Ego

autem cantabo fortitudinem tuam:
et exaltabo mane misericordiam tuam. Quia factus es susceptor meus:
et refugium meum in die tribulatio-
nis mee. Adiutor meus tibi psalla:
quia deus susceptor meus es: deus
meus misericordia mea. In fine pro
hijs qui comutabuntur in tituli i-
scriptoe ipsi dd in doctrina cu suctre-
dit mesopotamia syrie et sobal
et couertit ioab et percussit edom in
valle salinari duodeci milia.
Deus repulisti nos et destruxisti
nos: iratus es et misertus es
nobis. Commouisti terram et con-
turbasti eam: sana contritiones eius
quia comota est. Ostendisti populo
tuo dura: potasti nos vino compun-
ctionis. Dedisti metuentibus te signi-
ficationem: ut fugiant a facie arcus.
Ut liberentur dilecti tui: saluum fac
dextera tua et exaudi me. Deus locu-
tus est in sancto suo: letabor et par-
tibor sichimam: et conuallem taber-
naculorum metibor. Meus est gala-
ad et meus est manasses: et ephra-
im fortitudo capitis mei. Iuda rex
meus: moab olla spei mee. In y-
dumeam extendam calciamentu meum: michi alienigene subditi sunt.
Quis deducet me in ciuitatem muni-
tam: quis deducet me usq; in ydume-
am? Nonne tu deus qui repulisti
nos? et non egredieris deus in virtu-
tibus nostris. Da nobis auxilium
de tribulatione: et vana salus homi-
nis. In deo faciemus virtutem: et
ipse ad nichilu deducet tribulantes nos.
In fine in ymnis psalmus dauid
Exaudi deus deprecationem meam: intede orationi mee. A fi-
nibus terre ad te clamaui du anxiaret

HARTMANN SCHEDEL (1440–1514).
LIBER CHRONICARUM, 1493.

The Nuremberg chronicle is one of the
grandest productions of the first half-
century following the Western invention
of printing with movable type, known
as the incunable period. More than
600 woodblocks were cut to print
1,800 illustrations, with the same
cityscape, for instance, standing
in for both Lyon and Bologna.
The chronicle covers the full
range of history as it was then
known, from the Creation to the
present day, with blank pages
left toward the end for each
copy's owner to record further
significant events between
1493 and the Last Judgment.

Inc 2084 (A).
19 by 27 in. (when open).
Gift of Ward M. and
Miriam Coffin Canaday,
1954.

Ferraria

9

WORKS OF ARISTOTLE, THEOPHRASTUS, AND OTHER ANCIENT GREEK AUTHORS, CA. 1490.

ARISTOTLE. COLLECTED WORKS, 1495–1498.

After Gutenberg, the Italian printer Aldo Manuzio (known in Latin as Aldus Manutius) is regarded as the most important figure in the early history of printing in the West. Operating in Venice in the late 15th century, the Aldine Press pioneered portable, inexpensive versions of the classics that fueled Italian Humanism. The manuscript shown here provides a rare glimpse of the Aldine Press at work. Beyond the inky fingerprints endemic to any printing house, the manuscript shows the practice of "casting off"—estimating how the lines in a manuscript will correspond to the finished printed book. As can be seen from the printed page at right, the compositor performed this task quite accurately.

THIS PAGE
MS Gr 17.
13 by 9 in.
Gift of Harold T. White, Lucius Wilmerding, Augustin H. Parker, and William King Richardson, 1938.

OPPOSITE PAGE
WKR 2.5.5.
12½ by 9 in.
Bequest of William King Richardson, 1951.

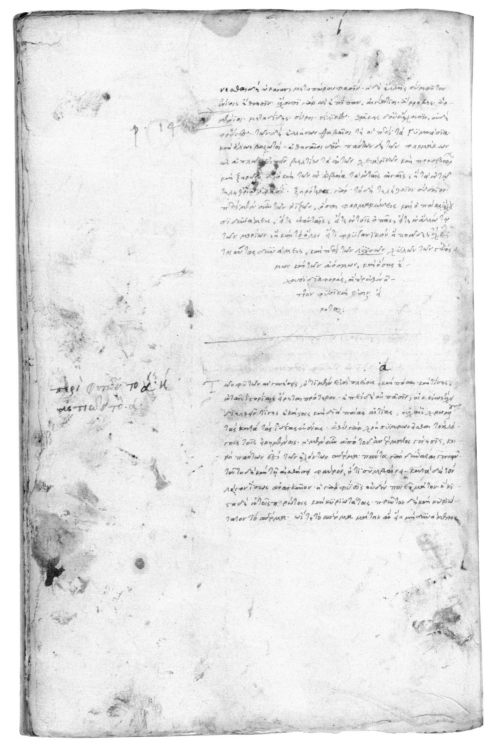

μικρὸν ἢ πολλὰς ἔχει τοιαύτας δυνάμεις, καὶ περὶ τῶν χυλῶν τῶν εὐόσμων, καὶ τῶν ἀόσμων, ποιοῦσι διαφορὰς, αἵπερ μάλιστα θεῖν ἧττον φυσικαὶ τῆς ῥίζης, πλείους μὲν εἰσιν αἱ δυνάμεις ἐν τῇ πλέω ζωῇ γὰρ ἢ δὲ μάλιστα αἱ φαρμακώδεις ὡς χρησιμώταται διαφέρουσι, τῶν τε μὴ περ πανταξῇ τῷ μὲν ἐν ταυτῷ ἔχῃ τῇ δυνάμ. ὡς περ εἴρηται μικρῷ πρότερον, ὡς δ' ἐν ὅλῳ παν αἱ πλεῖσται μὲν ἐν αὐτῇ τῇ ἔχουσι ἢ τῇ καρπῷ ἢ τῷ ὅτι ἐνιαχῆ ἢ ὧν τὸ φύλλον χ δομὴ ταύτας τε φυλλώδεις δυνάμεις τὰς πολλὰς πάσας καλοῦσιν οἱ ῥιζοτόμοι.

Ταῦτα μόνα τοῦ δεκάτου ἐν τοῖς ἀντιγράφοις εὑρήκαμεν, εἰ μὴ ἄρα τῷ ἐνάτῳ συγκεῖται τὰ λοιπά.

ΘΕΟΦΡΑΣΤΟΥ ΠΕΡΙ ΦΥΤΩΝ ΑΙΤΙΩΝ ΤΟ Α.

ΩΝ φυτῶν αἱ γενέσεις, ὅτι μὲν εἰσι πλείους, ἢ πόσαι, ἢ τίνα τῷ ἐν ταῖς ἱστορίαις εἴρηται πρότερον· ἐπεὶ δὲ οὐ πᾶσιν οἰκείως ἔχει διελθεῖν, τίνα ἑκάστοις ἢ διὰ ποίας αἰτίας οὐχ αἷς χρώμεθα τὰς κατὰ τὰς ἰδίας οὐσίας· αὐτὴ γὰρ χρὴ συμφωνεῖν τοὺς λόγους τῇ εἰρημένῃ ἡ μὲν γὰρ ἀπὸ τοῦ σπέρματος γένεσις, κοινὴ πάντων ὅσα τι ἔχοντων σπέρμα. πάντα γὰρ δύναται γενᾶν. εἰ τοῦτο ἢ τῇ αἰσθήσει φανερὸν ὅτι συμβαίνει κατὰ δὲ τοὺς λόγους ἴσως ἀναγκαῖον· ἡ γὰρ φύσις οὐδὲν ποιεῖ μάτην. ἥκιστα δὲ ἐν τοῖς πρώτοις καὶ κυριωτάτοις. πρῶτον δὲ καὶ κυριώτατον τὸ σπέρμα. ὥστε τὸ σπέρμα μάτην ἂν εἴη μὴ δυνάμενοις γεννᾶν. εἴπερ τούτου χάριν καὶ τὸ σπέρμα ἐπεὶ πρὸς τοῦτο πέφυκε

ὅπερ

PETER APIAN (1495–1552). *ASTRONOMICUM CAESAREUM*, 1540.

The volvelle, a paper instrument made of rotating disks, has been put to many uses in its history, but no work has used volvelles with such colorful virtuosity as *Astronomicum Caesareum*. Produced by the court astronomer to the Holy Roman Emperor Charles V, the book combines beautiful decoration with highly complex and delicate volvelles for calculating the positions of stars, planets, and comets.

Philip Hofer (Harvard Class of 1921) became the founding curator of the Department of Printing and Graphic Arts in 1938, placing on deposit at Harvard his already sizeable and important collection of books and manuscripts representing the history of printing and book illustration. He would continue in that role until 1968. His gifts of collections and endowments to sustain them, and his longstanding work in the library, are among the most significant contributions by any figure in Houghton history.

Typ 520.40.150, f. G3v (this page) and f. J1r.
19 by 27 in. (when open).
Gift of Philip Hofer, 1942.

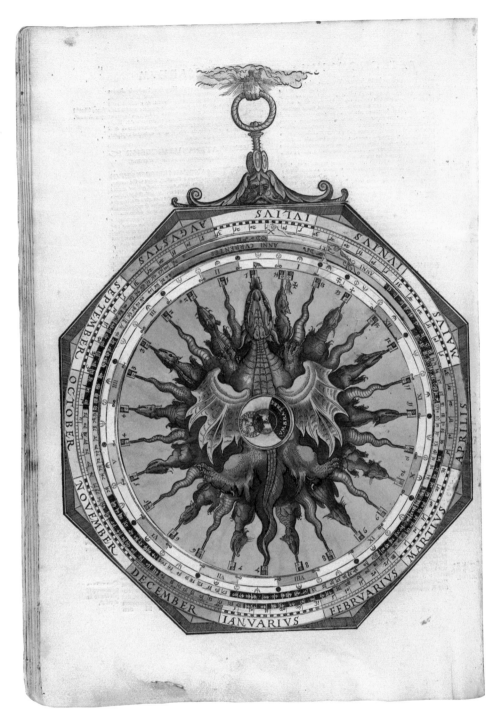

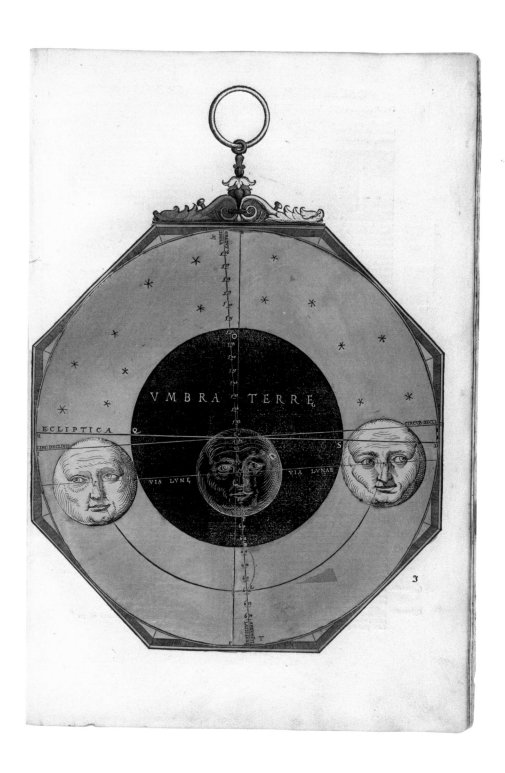

13

NICOLAUS COPERNICUS (1473–1543). *DE REVOLUTIONIBUS ORBIUM CŒLESTIUM*, 1543.

This simple diagram conveys one of the most profound discoveries in the history of science. It proposes for the first time a model of the heavens in which the Earth revolves around a stationary Sun instead of the reverse, the model accepted by religious and scientific authorities since the ancient Greeks. While careful to couch his argument as merely a theoretical construct useful for making calculations, Copernicus nonetheless sparked a century of astronomical discovery that completely rewrote our knowledge of the universe. This copy, in a binding dated 1552, comes from the outstanding science collection of David P. Wheatland (Harvard Class of 1922), the founding curator of the Harvard Collection of Historical Scientific Instruments.

GC5.C7906.543d.
11 by 8 in.
Gift of David P. Wheatland, 1971.

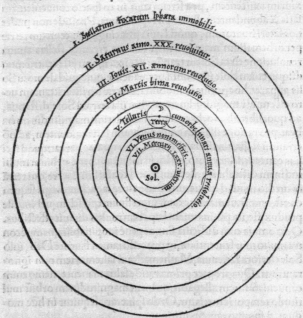

NICOLAI COPERNICI

net, in quo terram cum orbe lunari tanquam epicyclo contineri diximus. Quinto loco Venus nono mense reducitur. Sextum deniq; locum Mercurius tenet, octuaginta dierum spacio circū currens. In medio uero omnium residet Sol. Quis enim in hoc

pulcherimo templo lampadem hanc in alio uel meliori loco poneret, quàm unde totum simul possit illuminare? Siquidem non inepte quidam lucernam mundi, alij mentem, alij rectorem uocant. Trimegistus uisibilem Deum, Sophoclis Electra intuentē omnia. Ita profecto tanquam in solio re gali Sol residens circum agentem gubernat Astrorum familiam. Tellus quoq; minime fraudatur lunari ministerio, sed ut Aristoteles de animalibus ait, maximā Luna cū terra cognatione habet. Concipit interea à Sole terra, & impregnatur annuo partu. Inuenimus igitur sub
hac

ORONCE FINE (1494–1555).
LE SPHÈRE DU MONDE, 1549.

In contrast to Copernicus's groundbreaking heliocentric diagram opposite, cartographer and mathematician Oronce Fine presents a beautiful but conventionally geocentric view of the solar system. This elegant manuscript version of his popular astronomy textbook was presented to Henri II, the recently crowned King of France, in Fine's role as Royal Mathematician.

MS Typ 57.
10½ by 7 in.
Gift of Christian A. Zabriskie
and Philip Hofer, 1951.

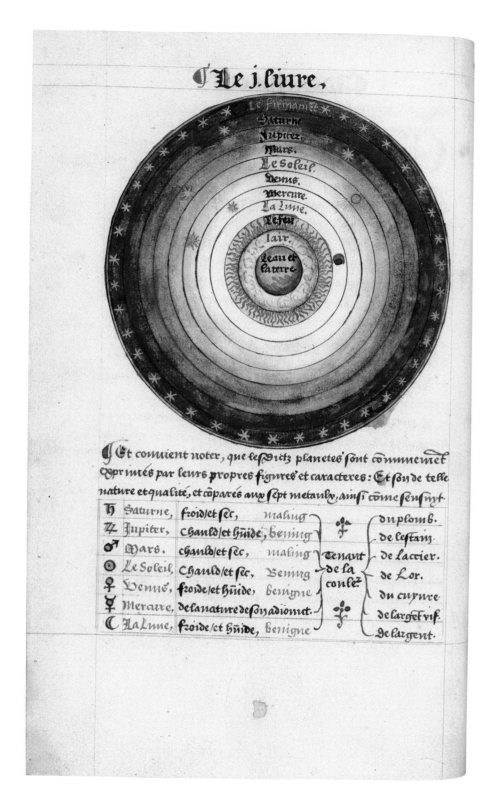

ELIZABETH I (1533–1603). LETTER TO KING EDWARD VI, 1552?

This letter is undated, but from the context it is likely that Princess Elizabeth wrote to her brother the King during a serious illness he suffered in 1552, when she was 19 years old. The superb penmanship she displays here owes to her training under Roger Ascham, a scholar, author, and professional scribe who tutored the future queen in Latin and Greek.

MS Typ 686.
12½ by 9 in.
Gift of Philip Hofer in memory of Andrew Oliver, 1983.

William Shakespeare
(1564–1616). *Mr. William Shakespeares comedies, histories, & tragedies, 1623.*

The First Folio of Shakespeare is widely regarded as the greatest landmark in English literature. Bringing together in one volume nearly all of Shakespeare's plays, half of which appear in print for the first time, the First Folio's heft and quality of production made the case for Shakespeare not merely as the author of ephemeral plays, but as a writer worthy of an enduring legacy. Its status as an iconic and highly prized book four centuries later testifies to its success in achieving that goal.

HEW 7.11.1.
13½ by 9 in.
Harry Elkins Widener Collection, 1915.

Mr. WILLIAM
SHAKESPEARES
COMEDIES,
HISTORIES, &
TRAGEDIES.

Published according to the True Originall Copies.

Martin Droeshout sculpsit London.

LONDON
Printed by Isaac Iaggard, and Ed. Blount. 1623.

THOMAS HARRIOT (1560–1621).
MERVEILLEUX ET ESTRANGE RAPPORT, 1590.

Thomas Harriot spent a year at the British colony on Roanoke Island and published a pamphlet describing the American Indian populations there in 1588. Two years later, the German publisher Theodore de Bry produced dramatically expanded illustrated editions in Latin, German, French, and English to an eager European audience. Based on the drawings of John White, an artist who accompanied Harriot to America, the illustrations present (for colonizers of the period) a comparatively humane and sympathetic depiction of the culture of the indigenous peoples they encountered.

US 19095.88.14.
13½ by 19 in. (when open).
Peter Paul Francis Degrand fund, 1941.

XVIII.

La facon de danser

de ceux de Virginia en
leurs festes solennelles.

Ls ont vn certain temps qu'ils tiennét vne gran-de feste & solennelle , à laquelle viennét de tous costez & se trouuét leurs prochains voisins , cha-cun d'eux accoustré à sa mode le plus e-strangement qu'il peut , & marqué sur le dos de marques selon le lieu d'ou il est. Il se faict donques vn grand circuit ou ils s'assemblent, planté en rond de pieces de bois taillees en marmousets aians la teste comme vne nonnain voilee. S'estans mis en rond, ils sautent, dansent, chantent, & font les plus estranges grimasses dond ils se peuuent auiser. Au milieu du circuit y a trois des plus belles filles qu'on a sceu choisir, lesquelles s'embrassans l'une l'au-tre, se tournent comme en dansant. Tout ce mistere se faict apres le Soleil couché, pour la grande chaleur du jour. Ceux qui ont acheué leurs sauts, sortent du circuit, & y en entre des autres , tant que tout soit fini , puis se mettent à banqueter ainsi qu'il est representé par la fi-gure XVI.

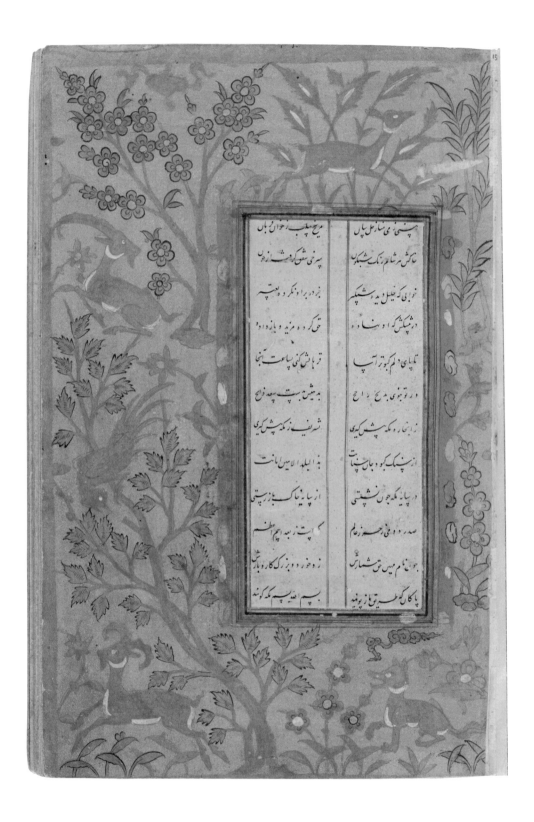

AFẒAL AL-DĪN SHIRVĀNĪ KHĀQĀNĪ
(CA. 1126–1198).
TUḤFAT AL-ʿIRĀQAYN, 1604.

Tuḥfat al-ʿIrāqayn (in English, The gift of the two Iraqs) describes the poet Khāqānī's pilgrimage to Mecca in 1156–1160. This manuscript, created nearly 450 years after the poem's composition, displays virtuosic calligraphy and illumination. The miniature on this page spills out of its frame in a way that reflects the action-filled hunting scene it depicts, while the more muted but no less finely drawn plants and animals on the left provide a subtler background for the text.

MS Typ 536, f. 14v (this page) and f. 15r.
11 by 15 in. (when open).
Fund for Printing and Graphic Arts given by Philip Hofer, 1966.

The Little Gidding Harmony, 1630.

The small religious community formed at Little Gidding in Huntingdonshire, England, in the 1620s is today best remembered for its Gospel Harmonies. Seeking to blend the four gospel accounts of the life of Jesus into a single narrative, the women of the community cut apart printed Bibles into pieces sometimes as small as a single word. They then pasted these fragments into a new book with additional engraved illustrations. This delicate work both created a devotional book unlike any other used in the period, and was itself an act of religious devotion. King Charles I was so taken with this book that he borrowed it for a time, and left his own notes in it, later commissioning from Little Gidding a Harmony of his own.

A 1275.5.
14½ by 21 in. (when open).
Henry Saltonstall Howe fund, 1941.

is this that speaketh blasphemies? Who can for
7 giue sinnes, but God alone?
8 And immediatly when Iesus perceiued in his spirit
that they so reasoned within themselues And Iesus know
ing their thoughts, hee answering, said vnto them Wher
fore thinke you euill in your hearts?
9 Whether is it easier to say to the sicke of the palsie,
Thy sinnes be forgiuen thee: or to say, Arise, and take vp
thy bed and walke?
10 But that ye may know that the Sonne of man hath
power on earth to forgiue sinnes, (he saith to the sicke of
the palsie,)

11 I say vnto thee, Arise, and take vp thy bed, and goe
thy way into thine house.
12 And immediatly hee arose, vp before them, and
tooke vp the bed, wherein he lay, and went forth before
them all, and departed to his owne house, glorifieng
God But when the multitudes sawe it, they marueiled, and
26 And they were all amazed, and they glorified God,
which had giuen such power vnto men
and were filled with feare, saying, We haue seene strange
things to day.
Wee neuer saw it on this fashion.

*xxiii.
And after these things, he went forth, againe by
the Sea-side, and all the multitude resorted
vnto him, and he taught them.
9 And as Iesus passed forth from thence, he saw a
man a Publicane named Leui, the son of Alphæus
sitting at the receipt of custome: named Matthew, and
he said vnto him, Follow me.
28 And he left all, rose vp, and followed him And Leui
made him a great feast in his own house.
10 And it came to passe as Iesus sate at meat in the
house, behold, many Publicanes and sinners came and
sate also together
with Iesus and his disciples: for there were many, and
they followed him.
16 And when the Scribes and Pharisees saw him eat
and drinke with publicanes and sinners they murmured
And said vnto his disciples,
Why doe yee eate with Publicanes and sinners? How
is it that your Master he eateth and drinketh with

Mathew IX
Luke. ii.
Mrc. V.

pub and sinners?
hee answering, said vnto them, They that are
whole need not a Physician, but they that are sicke.
13 But goe yee and learne what that meaneth, I will
haue mercy and not sacrifice: For I am not come to call
the righteous, but sinners to repentance.
14 Then came to him the disciples of Iohn,
18 And the disciples of Iohn and of the Pharisees vsed
to fast: and they come, and say vnto him, Why doe the dis
ciples of Iohn fast often, and make prayers, and like
disciples of the Pharisees: but thy disciples
fast not? But eate and drinke?
15 And Iesus sayd vnto them, can the children of the
bride-chamber mourne, And fast, while the Bridegroome
is with them?
as long as the bridegrome is with them they
35 But the dayes will come, when the Bridegroom
shall be taken away from them, and then shall they fast in
those dayes.

JOHN DOWNAME (d. 1652).
THE CHRISTIAN WARFARE, 1634.

John Harvard, an English minister educated at Cambridge University, moved to Boston in 1637 and died the following year. His bequest to the fledgling college recently founded in Cambridge, Massachusetts (then known as Newtowne), of half the value of his estate and his library of some 400 volumes was significant enough that the college was named in his memory in 1639. After a 1764 fire devastated the Harvard College library, this lone survivor from John Harvard's library has held a place of honor, and it was transported into Widener Library when it opened in 1915 in a ceremonial procession led by the president of the university.

STC 7137.
13½ by 18 in. (when open).
Bequest of John Harvard,
1638.

THE FRONT
OPENED.

THe *Christian Souldier* in IEHOVAH's *might*,
Watching in Prayer, manly keepes his *station*,
And in his compleat Armes *Diuinely* bright,
Prepares to make resistance in *tentation*.

Sathan (chiefe Captaine in this hellish field)
His *poysoned fiery Darts* against him flingeth;
Which catch't and quench't with *Faith's vnpierced Shield*;
Hits, falls, and *only tryes*; no damage bringeth.

The World (Leiuetenant Generall in this fight)
In *Harlots habit*, fawningly allures him
To sinfull, shamefull swaruing from all right,
This done, *Wealth, Honours, Pleasures*, she assures him.

Which he contemning; full of *Spleene and Hate*,
Shee turnes her *Smiles to Frownes*, nought else now breathing
But (Tyrant-like) Fire, Faggot, Sword, and Bate,
Gibbets and Gayles, no crueltie out-leauing.

The *Flesh*, the *last*, the *worst* of hellish traine,
When outward *Foes* assault him with *tentation*,
Traytrously yeelds, allur'd with *Worldly gaine*;
Him also moties to yeeld, and quit his station.

Fayling in this; *Treason* he turnes to *Rage*;
And like a Captaine *old* and *subtile* places
Legions of lawlesse Lusts, which he doth wage,
To fight against *Him* and his *sauing Graces*.

'gainst all these powers of Hell *Christs Champion stands*,
And though sometimes his strength fainteth and faileth,
Through fierce encounters of these *horrid bands*;
In his *Grand Leader's might* he still preuayleth :

Vntill at last full *Victory* he gaines,
Treads, tramples on their *Crests* with feet victorious,
In *triumph* leads them *captiue*, and obtaines
An heauenly *Crowne*, Royall, Immortall, Glorious.

F. D.

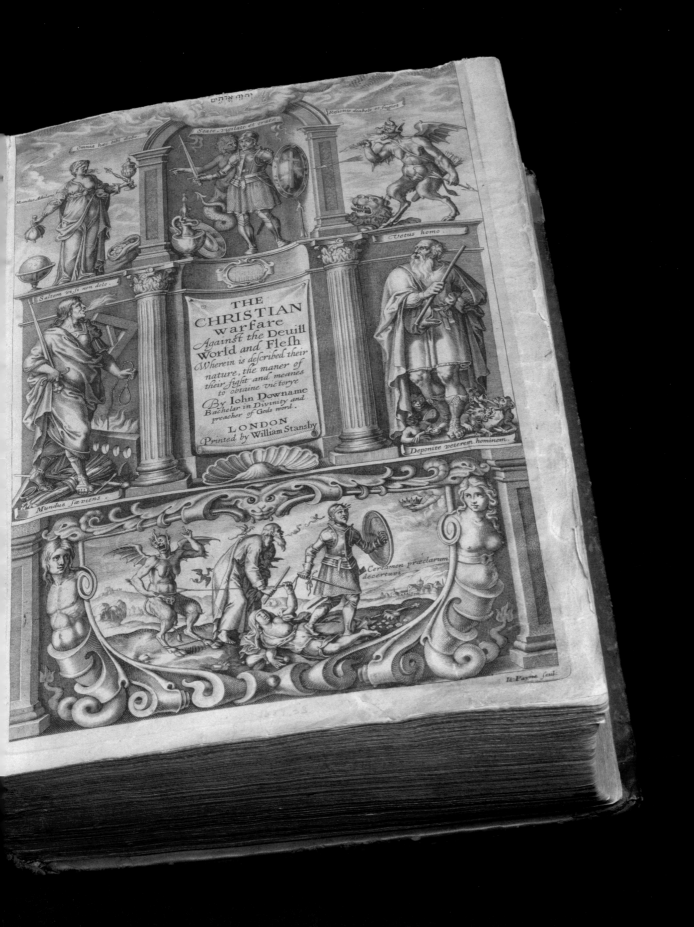

Nicholas Comberford (active 1612–1670). Portolan chart of the New World, 1659.

A portolan chart depicts the world as a
sailor sees it, with great oceans bounded
by coastlines notable primarily for the
places a ship may put in to port. This
map is the product of a group of English
mapmakers called the Thames School,
whose influence on cartography grew in
the 17th and 18th century in tandem with
Britain's increasing dominance of the seas.
It came to Houghton in 1951 as part of a
large and important collection of maps
belonging to the Prince of Liechtenstein.

MS Eng 1449.
Manuscript on vellum. 23 by 17½ in.
(In full on facing page, detail this page.)
Gift of Curt H. Reisinger and
Stephen W. Phillips, 1951.

NOVA ANGLIA

VIRGINIA

FLORIDA

HONDVRAS

TERRA FIRMA

POPAYAN

MAR DEL ZVR

CIVIANA

PERV

27

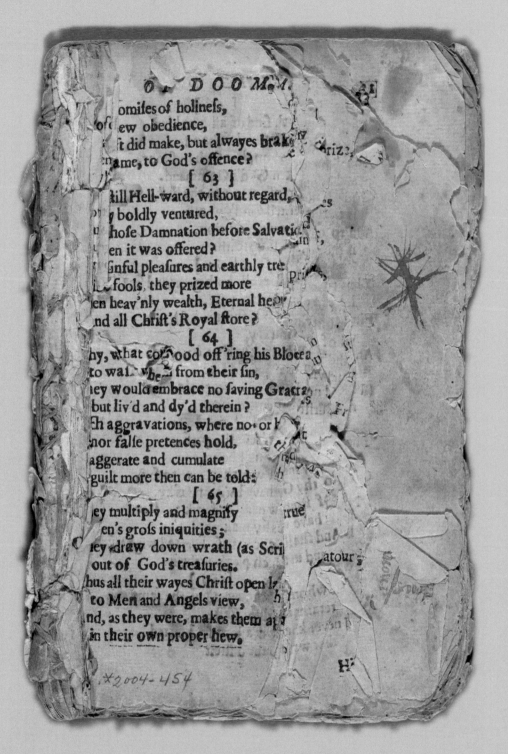

ꞋEWANGLESTE D-NAṬORA DA-ꞋLAYME, 18TH CENTURY.

This manuscript was created for an Assyrian Christian, and is small enough to be carried by its owner at all times. It contains a collection of charms, or prayers for protection, to various saints. The illustration here depicts Mar Gewargis (St. George) and the dragon.

MS Syriac 156.
4½ by 6 in. (when open).
Deposited by the Harvard Semitic Museum, ca. 1959.

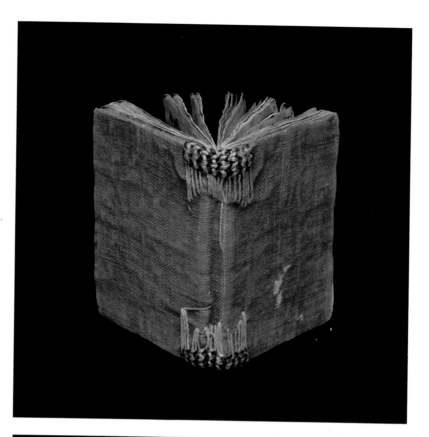

FIRDAWSĪ (CA. 940–1020). *SHĀHNĀMAH*, 1718–1721.

The *Shāhnāmah* or the Book of kings, the great epic of Persian mythology and history, is the world's longest poem by a single author. The calligrapher who created this manuscript in the early 18th century can be traced to Lahore in modern-day Pakistan and may himself be depicted on the left of the illumination on this page.

MS Persian 78.
14 by 21 in. (when open).
Gift of Philip Hofer, 1953.

PSYLLOGRAPHY, EARLY 19TH CENTURY.

This book preserves the work of an unidentified German shoemaker who turned his vocational skills with knife and scissors toward the craft of silhouette making. Despite the elegance of these designs, silhouettes draw their name from an allusion to cheapness. The stringent austerity measures of Étienne de Silhouette, treasury minister under Louis XV, led to his name being associated with this less expensive alternative to painted portraiture.

MS Typ 82.
8 by 6½ in.
Gift of Edward P. Hamilton, 1951.

HISTORIES
OR
TALES of paſt Times:

VIZ.

I. The Little Red Riding-hood.
II. The Fairy.
III. The Blue Beard.
IV. The Sleeping Beauty in the Wood.
V. The Maſter Cat, or Puſs in Boots.
VI. *Cinderilla*, or the Little Glaſs Slipper.
VII. *Riquet a la Houpe.*
VIII. Little *Poucet*, and his Brothers.
IX. The Diſcreet Princeſs, or the Adventures of *Finetta*.

With MORALS.

By M. PERRAULT.

Tranſlated into Engliſh.

LONDON:
Printed for J. POTE, at Sir *Iſaac New-ton's* Head, near *Suffolk-ſtreet, Charing-croſs*; and R. MONTAGU, the Corner of *Great Queen-ſtreet,* near *Drury-lane.* M.DCC.XXIX.

CHARLES PERRAULT (1628–1703).
HISTORIES, OR TALES OF PAST TIMES, 1729.

Some of the world's most enduring and well-known fairy tales, including "Little Red Riding Hood," "Sleeping Beauty," and "Cinderella," were introduced into English literature with the publication of this volume. Children's books are often read to pieces and discarded, and this seems to have been the case with this work; Houghton's copy is the only one known to survive.

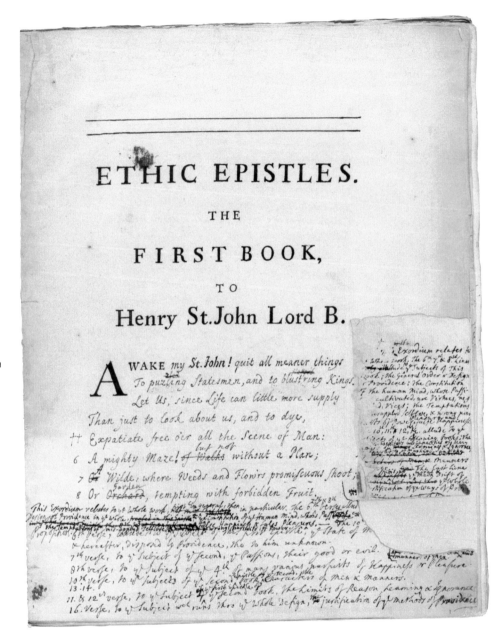

SAMUEL JOHNSON (1709–1784). *A SHORT SCHEME FOR COMPILING A NEW DICTIONARY OF THE ENGLISH LANGUAGE,* 1746.

In 1746, Samuel Johnson was commissioned by a consortium of London publishers to produce a comprehensive English dictionary. Johnson's first task was to produce this manuscript, in which he set out the principles that would guide his work. This essay was intended to serve as an advertisement for the finished dictionary, but Johnson would not complete the monumental intellectual labor required until 1755. Johnson's choices of which words to include, his determination of their proper spelling and definition, and the authors whose writing he chose to illustrate their meaning, played a crucial role in shaping the English language as it is spoken today.

This manuscript came to Houghton in 2003 as part of the Donald and Mary Hyde Collection of Samuel Johnson, the world's most comprehensive collection of books and manuscripts relating to the life and writings of Johnson, as well as his circle of friends and associates.

MS Hyde 50 (38).
8 by 6 in.
Bequest of Mary Hyde Eccles, 2003.

MELESINDA MUNBEE (B. CA. 1744).
A COLLECTION OF VARIOUS KINDS OF POETRY, 1749–1750.

We know regrettably little about the girl who penned this book with such a skilled hand at the age of five. We do know, however, that the practice of penmanship and the making of commonplace books were both important parts of the education of the children of the elite in 18th century England. Houghton's collections hold numerous other examples of commonplace books—transcriptions of particularly interesting or edifying passages from one's reading—but no others from a compiler so precocious.

MS Eng 768.
7 by 11 in. (when open).
Norton Perkins fund, 1949.

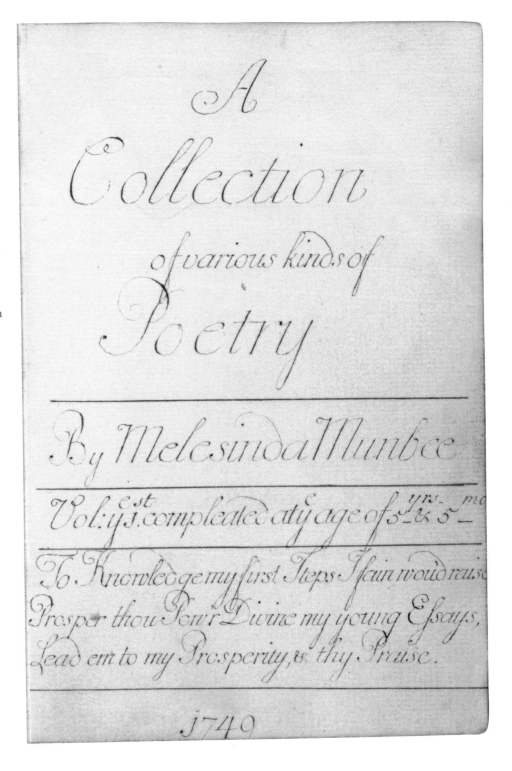

A Sapphic Ode.

Found in ye Cabinet of a young Oxxonian
after his decease, who was the Author
of ye Rules for writing polite Poetry.

Curse on ye sounding Temple, & ye Temple
And heavens strict precepts, are th' unjust pretension
Must I for ever listen to ye Fooliries
        of driveling dotards.

PHILLIS WHEATLEY (1753–1784). *AN ELEGIAC POEM ON THE DEATH OF . . . GEORGE WHITEFIELD*, 1770.

The girl who would become known as Phillis Wheatley was kidnapped and sold into slavery at the age of seven. She was purchased by John Wheatley of Boston as a servant for his wife and named for the ship which brought her to the Colonies. Unusually for an enslaved person of the time, Phillis was taught by the Wheatley family to read and write, and she quickly turned her hand to the writing of poetry, including a poem addressed to the students of Harvard. This, her first separately published work, memorializes George Whitefield, a galvanizing preacher who helped ignite the Great Awakening. The success of this elegy made possible the publication in London in 1773 of *Poems on various subjects, religious and moral*, the first volume of poetry published by an African American woman.

AC7.W5602.770e.
8 by 5½ in.
Gift of the Seven Gables Bookshop, 1966.

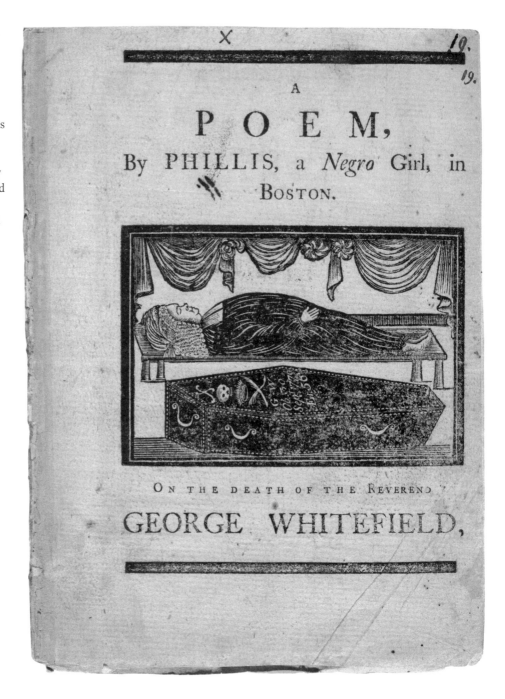

Diplomatic relations between France and the United States, so crucial to American independence, became strained after the French Revolution, and France viewed with alarm the increasing ties between the U.S. and Great Britain, which culminated in the Jay Treaty of 1794. James Monroe, appointed ambassador to France by George Washington just before the signing of the Jay Treaty, strongly opposed this shift in American alliances. With pro-British forces led by Alexander Hamilton ascendant in Washington's cabinet, Monroe grew increasingly alienated from administration policy and began advancing his own agenda, leading to his dismissal from the post in 1796. Stung by the slight, Monroe published this scathing critique of Washington and his administration the following year. Unsurprisingly, Washington swiftly obtained a copy and read it with interest, responding extensively in the margins. Washington's tone throughout is clear from his reply to Monroe's very first sentence. Monroe writes, "In the month of May, 1794, I was invited by the President of the United States, through the Secretary of State, to accept the office of minister plenipotentiary to the French Republic." Washington ripostes, "After several attempts had failed to obtain a more eligible character."

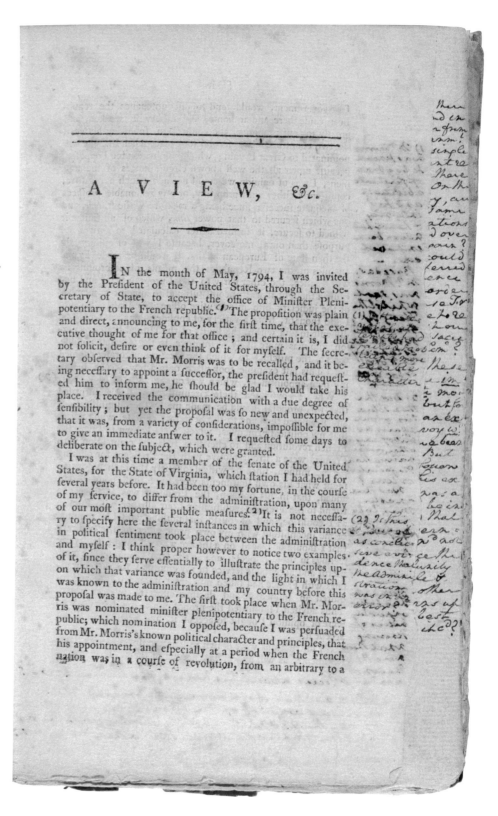

David Garrick (1717–1779). Commemorative medal designed by John Kirk, 1776.

Given Garrick's monumental importance to the English stage of the 18th century and his central role in Samuel Johnson's circle of friends, it is no surprise that Houghton's collections are rich with material documenting his life and career. This medal was struck to mark his retirement from acting at the age of 59.

MS Thr 792 (13).
Bronze. 1½ in.
Fredric Woodbridge Wilson Collection
of Theater, Dance and Music, 2010.

Johann Ludwig Wernhard Fäsch (ca. 1738–1778). Four portraits of performers in the Drury Lane Theatre and the Comedie Française, ca. 1760–1778.

The Swiss miniaturist Johann Fäsch is best known for the portraits he made of the luminaries of the London and Paris stage in the 1760s and 1770s. He is the first artist known to have drawn his portraits during theatrical performances, so these images provide a particularly valuable glimpse inside London's Drury Lane Theatre at the moment that David Garrick was cementing his reputation as the greatest English actor of the 18th century.

MS Thr 645.
Graphite, watercolor, and gold paint on vellum.
4 by 4 in. Source unknown.

Mr GARRICK
in the Character of LUSIGNAN
in Zara.

ARISTE
Dans la Pupille.

Mrs BARRY and Mr GARRICK
in the Characters of VIOLANTE and D.FELIX.
in the Wonder.

VICTORINE   VANDER fils
Dans le Philosophe sans le sçavoir

41

WILLIAM BLAKE (1757–1827). *EUROPE A PROPHECY*, 1794.

William Blake's combined skills as an illustrator and a poet, and the intensity of his artistic vision underlying both, enabled him to produce works so unlike anything else that they were underappreciated in his lifetime. Today, however, Blake is regarded as a genius whose work presaged the modern artist's book. The frontispiece to *Europe a prophecy*, known as "The Ancient of Days," is one of Blake's best-known images and showcases his dramatic compositions and vibrant colors. Thirteen copies of the work are known to survive, many, including this one, uniquely hand-colored by Blake himself.

Typ 6500.41c.
14½ by 10½ in.
Gift of Ruth Underhill White, 1964.

42

Luigi Cherubini (1760–1842).
Ouverture für das Clavier: aus der Oper Elisa,
ca. 1803.

Actor and playwright Alois Senefelder (1771–1834) was the inventor of lithography. After bemoaning the costs associated with printing his works, he experimented with various alternatives and finally settled on what he called "chemical printing," in which he marked a stone with greasy ink, then coated the surface with a mixture of water, acid and gum arabic. The inked surface could then be printed directly to paper. After continuing to experiment and improve the process, Senefelder went to London where he received patent letters in June 1801.

He then founded his own printing company in Vienna, the Chemische Druckerey, in July 1803. This extraordinary early example was created in 1803, shortly after the founding of the company.

This piece is just one of the thousands of artifacts in the Harvard Theatre Collection's John Milton and Ruth Neils Ward Collection, comprised of books, scores, librettos, and other materials relating to public performances of music and dance.

44

2008TW-270.
9½ by 26½ (when open).
Gift of John Milton and Ruth Neils Ward, 2008.

John James Audubon (1785–1851). Carolina Parakeet, 1811.

Houghton Library holds 116 of Audubon's early drawings of birds and other animals.

Audubon was born in Haiti, raised in France, and emigrated to America in 1803, where he quickly developed a keen interest in American wildlife. Audubon composed his drawings from fresh-killed specimens. This drawing is one of three now-extinct species represented in the collection. Audubon's studies would lead to the publication of his magnum opus, *The birds of America* (1827–1838), known as the "elephant folio" for its great size, of which Houghton holds two copies.

MS Am 21 (88).
Watercolor, pastel, graphite, and ink on paper. 17 by 11 in.
Bequest of Joseph Y. Jeanes, 1930.

This early draft of Keats's "To Autumn" contains the poet's corrections, and is one of two manuscripts of the poem in Houghton's collection.

Houghton Library's collection of Keats's manuscripts, books written by and belonging to him, objects, and secondary source material is the largest in the world, preserving nearly three-quarters of his surviving manuscript poetry. The majority of the collection was given to Harvard by two collectors: the poet and philanthropist Amy Lowell (whose own important library and manuscript collection are also at Houghton) and Arthur A. Houghton Jr., whose gift of funds gave the library its name. The collection is displayed in the Keats Room on the library's second floor.

MS Keats 2.27.
9½ by 8 in.
Bequest of Amy Lowell, 1925.

QUADRILLING: A FAVOURITE SONG, 1821.

Befitting an institution with a strong department of Printing and Graphic Arts, Houghton Library holds some fascinating examples of music as art. William Hawkes Smith was an early amateur lithographic printer who was drawn to the ease with which one could write on stone. This score, which he printed in 1821 in Birmingham, England, shows how well lithography can integrate music with text and illustrations into an irresistible visual tour de force.

M1977.H7 Q3 1821.
14 by 10 in.
Gift of John Milton and Ruth Neils Ward, 2010.

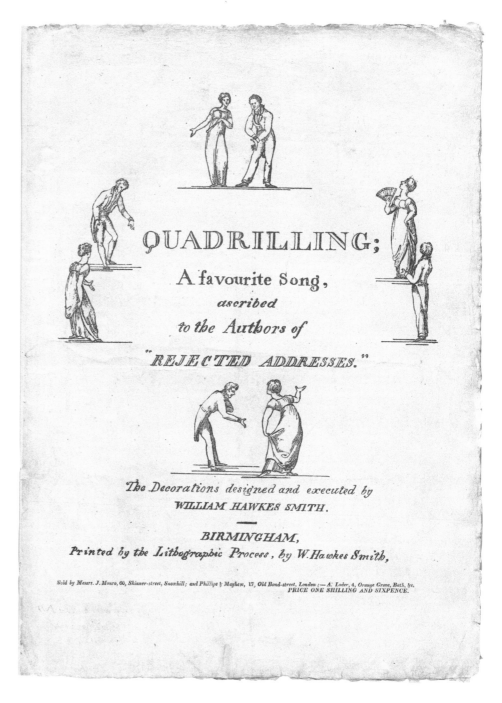

Air Le Balancér

Run neighbours, run, all London is quadrilling it; Order and Sobri-e-ty are dos à dos
This is the day for toeing it, and heeling it; All are promenading it from high to low

King Al-mack, with his Star and Garter Coteries   Never did anticipate such democratic votaries.
Courtiers & Citizens are flirting with Terpsichore, The town is an amphitheatre for capering & kickery.

Run, neighbours, run, all London is quadrilling it; Order and Sobriety are dos à dos.
This is the day for toeing it and heeling it; All are promenading it from high to low.

Dames, Cavaliers too, unwilling all to stand alone,
Thinking practice requisite to do things right;
Like Harlequin & Columbine, rehearsing with lord Pantaloon,
Meet slyly in the morning to prepare for night.—
Paine's first set invented to delight us, is
Danced at St James's, St Giles's, and St Vitus's —
Dandies turning figurants, conceive they've made a clever hit,
And Widows weighing thirty stone, attempt to pas-de-zephyr it
                    (Cho)   Run, neighbours, run, &c.

CHARLOTTE (1816–1855) AND BRANWELL BRONTË (1817–1848). JUVENILIA, 1829–1830.

Isolated at their home in West Yorkshire, the Brontë siblings formed what their father termed "a society among themselves," writing stories, plays, and poems set in imaginary worlds. Using small scraps of paper, they created tiny handsewn booklets, often mimicking real books and magazines. The nine books in Houghton's collection, acquired by poet and collector Amy Lowell, were written in miniature lettering by Charlotte Brontë and her brother Branwell, and are among only twenty examples that survive.

Books 1–6 by Charlotte Brontë, 1829–1830;
books 7–9 by Patrick Branwell Brontë, 1829.
Each book approximately 2 by 1½ in.
MS Lowell 1. Bequest of Amy Lowell, 1925.

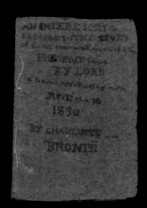

1

2

3

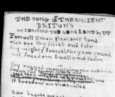

4

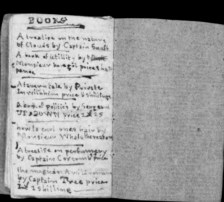

5

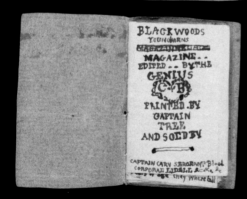

6

7

8

9

EDWARD LEAR (1812–1888).
***BLUE PARROT* [LEAR'S MACAW],**
1832.

Houghton's collection of the papers
and drawings of English author and
artist Edward Lear is the largest in
existence. Remembered primarily
for his nonsense verse, Lear was an
accomplished painter and natural
historian. As a teenager, he studied
parrots at the London Zoo, and at age
twenty he published the critically-
acclaimed *Illustrations of the family
of Psittacidae, or parrots* (1832). The
library holds over 80 of Lear's parrot
drawings, along with thousands of
illustrations for his poetry, landscape
drawings, and other works.

MS Typ 55.9 (22).
Graphite and watercolor drawing.
21½ by 15 in.
Gift of W. B. O. Field, 1942.

Aleksandr Sergeyevich Pushkin (1799–1837). *Moriu* ["To the sea"], 1824.

Following the drowning of Lord Byron in April 1824, Prince Petr Viazemsky encouraged Pushkin to compose a poem in Byron's honor. Pushkin, somewhat scathingly, replied, ". . . I am very glad of his death as a sublime subject for poetry. As Byron's youth faded, so did his genius . . . I promise you, however, some scribblings on His Excellency's death" (Malmstad, *Pushkin and his friends,* Cambridge [Mass.]: Houghton Library, 1987, p. 28).

The unparalleled Kilgour Collection of Russian Literature, amassed by Bayard Livingston Kilgour Jr. (Harvard Class of 1927), given to Houghton in 1952 and expanded each year through dedicated endowment funds, is especially strong in the work of Pushkin.

MS Russ 4.
12½ by 8 in.
Gift of Bayard L. Kilgour Jr., 1953.

THAI FORTUNE-TELLING MANUSCRIPT, EARLY 19TH CENTURY.

Four-page spreads in this accordion-folded, unfinished manuscript depict the animal for a specific year, and can be used to determine major life events, such the outcome of a rice crop, a marriage, or financial success, based on the birth day and month of the user. In 1844, Maria Revere Balestier, wife to the first American consul to Singapore, sent the manuscript to her friend Eliza Morton Quincy, the wife of Harvard president Josiah

Quincy. The manuscript returned to Harvard in 1944, along with a large gift of material from biographer, editor, historian, and poet Mark Antony DeWolfe Howe, the husband of Quincy's great-granddaughter.

MS Typ 439.
Each panel 14½ by 5 in. Gift of M. A. DeWolfe Howe, 1944.

RALPH WALDO EMERSON (1803–1882). *WIDE WORLD 1*, 1820.

Transcendentalist Ralph Waldo Emerson (Harvard Class of 1821) seems to have been a philosopher from the beginning. Emerson kept this journal and commonplace book as a 17-year-old Harvard senior, recording his thoughts on his everyday life, readings, and what he called his "imaginings," all signed using his pseudonym "Junio." On this page, Emerson sketched a view of his room in Hollis Hall.

The Emerson papers, first deposited at Houghton by family members in 1942, contain Emerson's correspondence, notebooks and journals, lectures and sermons, as well as the papers of family members, including hundreds of letters and the intriguing diaristic "almanacks" of Emerson's erudite aunt, Mary Moody Emerson. Members of the Transcendentalist circle represented in Houghton collections include the Alcott family, Margaret Fuller, siblings James and Sarah Freeman Clarke, Henry David Thoreau, and others.

MS Am 1280H (2).
8½ by 6½ in.
Presented by The Ralph Waldo Emerson Memorial Association in honor of the fiftieth birthday of the Houghton Library, 1991.

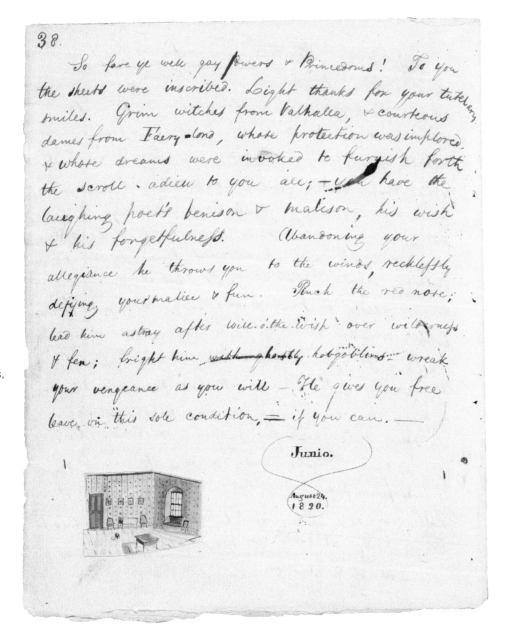

Along with the archives of authors' manuscripts and published works, Houghton holds substantial collections of authors' libraries, including those of Emily Dickinson, Sarah Orne Jewett, William James, Elizabeth Bishop, John Updike, and many others. Books belonging to novelist Herman Melville frequently contain heavy marginalia, such as the notes found in this book, one of only a few known specific copies of sources Melville consulted while writing *Moby-Dick* (1851). The cetology chapters of *Moby-Dick* borrow heavily from Beale, which Melville studied carefully. On this page Melville has written, "There is some sort of mistake in the drawing of Fig. 2. The tail part is wretchedly cropped & dwarfed, & looks altogether unnatural. The head is good."

33

CHAPTER II.

HABITS OF THE SPERM WHALE.

Fig. 1.   *Fig.* 2. ✗   *Fig.* 3.

IT is a matter of great astonishment that the consideration of the habits of so interesting, and in a commercial point of view of so important an animal, should have been so entirely neglected, or should have excited so little curiosity among the numerous, and many of them competent observers, that of late years must have possessed the most abundant and the most convenient opportunities of witnessing their habitudes. I am not vain enough to pretend that the few following pages include a perfect sketch of this subject, as regards the sperm whale; but I flatter myself that somewhat of novelty and originality will be found justly ascribable to the observations I have put together; they are at all events the fruit of long and attentive consideration.—For convenience of description, the habits of this animal are given under the heads of feeding, swimming, breathing, etc.

✗ There is some sort of mistake in the drawing of Fig: 2. The tail part is wretchedly cropped & dwarfed, & looks altogether unnatural. The head is good.

c 2

DAGUERREOTYPES, CA. 1840–1860.

The Harrison D. Horblit Collection of Early Photography, compiled by bibliophile and philanthropist Harrison D. Horblit (Harvard Class of 1933), includes over 3,000 daguerreotypes, 105 ambrotypes, 84 tintypes, 3,100 paper prints, 370 albums and photographically illustrated books, three early cameras, and many reference works, making it one of the most important collections of its kind.

The first widely available photographic process, daguerreotypes were made with mirror-finished, silver-plated sheets of copper, and usually displayed in elaborate leather, velvet, and gilt cases. For approximately two dollars, loved ones could be photographed by any of the hundreds of practicing daguerreotypists across the country.

Houghton's collection includes hundreds of portraits of anonymous men, women, children, Civil War soldiers, and miscellaneous scenes, accessed through the Printing & Graphic Arts department and carefully monitored by a team of Harvard's photograph conservators.

FACING PAGE UPPER LEFT:
John McElroy.
Boy on sofa with dog, ca. 1850.
TypDAG2079.
Sixth plate daguerreotype,
4 by 3½ by ½ in.

FACING PAGE UPPER RIGHT:
Two girls, between 1840 and 1860.
TypDAG1875.
Sixth plate daguerreotype.
4 by 3½ by 1 in.

FACING PAGE LOWER LEFT:
American School.
Two men, one holding a saw
and an axe and one holding a
hammer, between 1840 and 1860.
TypDAG2084.
Sixth plate daguerreotype,
4 by 3½ by 1 in.

FACING PAGE LOWER RIGHT:
Attributed to Platt D. Babbitt.
View of tourists at Prospect Point,
Niagara Falls, ca. 1855.
TypDAG2849.
Whole plate daguerreotype,
9 by 7 by 1 in.

Gift of Jean M. Horblit, 1995.

Pauline Viardot (1821–1910).

French singer, composer, and artist Pauline García Viardot was renowned for her opera performances in roles requiring a wide range of vocal and acting skills. After retiring from the stage in 1863, Viardot turned to teaching and composing; Franz Liszt declared her a composer of genius. Fluency in six languages aided her close friendships with many leading artists of her time, including George Sand, Ivan Turgenev, Frédéric Chopin, Jenny Lind, and Clara Schumann.

The Viardot papers include correspondence with family and friends, drawings, literary and musical compositions and printed scores. The composition *Stornello*, from *Le dernier sorcier* (1857), is in an album of 96 of Viardot's pieces for voice and piano.

Viardot's striking self-portrait, from a collection of her theatrical costume designs, portraits of friends, and other sketches, is pictured at right.

Stornello. MS Mus 264 (97).
10½ by 18½ in.
Ruth N. and John M. Ward fund, the Amy Lowell fund, the Frank E. Chase bequest, the John M. Kasdan fund, and the Bayard Livingston and Kate Gray Kilgour fund, 2011.

Album. MS Mus 264 (356).
11½ by 8½ in.

OTIS ALLEN BULLARD (1816–
1853), ARTIST.
THE DICKINSON CHILDREN,
CA. 1840.

EMILY DICKINSON (1830–1886).
*BAFFLED FOR JUST A DAY OR
TWO—*, 1860.

Houghton Library's Emily
Dickinson collection is the largest
in the world, containing over one
thousand autograph poems and 300
letters, Dickinson's writing table,
the Dickinson family library, and
many more objects of significance
associated with the poet, on display in
the library's Emily Dickinson Room.
This portrait of Emily Dickinson at
about age nine (on the left), with her
siblings Austin and Lavinia, is one
of only three known likenesses of
Dickinson made in her lifetime.

From a young age, as evidenced by
the portrait, Dickinson loved books
and flowers, and remained an avid
gardener and reader throughout her
life. Among the library's collection
of manuscripts is this poem sent to
friends Josiah Gilbert and Elizabeth
Chapin Holland, onto which
Dickinson affixed a rosebud.

Dickinson Room. Oil on canvas; 28 by 24 in.
Gift of Gilbert H. Montague, class of 1901,
in happy memory of Amy Angell Collier
Montague, 1950.

Baffled for just a day or two.
Embarrassed — not afraid.
Encounter in my garden
An unexpected Maid!
She beckons, and the Woods start.
She nods, and all begin —
Surely — such a country
I was never in!

Emilie

MS Am 1118.2 (17a). 6 by 4 in. Bequest of Theodora V. W. Ward, 1974.

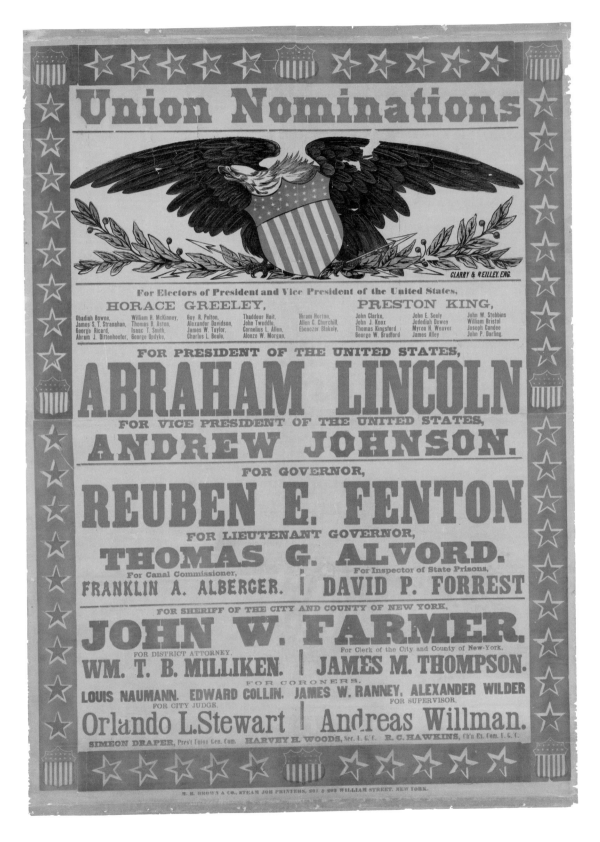

FREDERICK DOUGLASS (1818–1895). LETTER TO CHARLES SUMNER, APRIL 29, 1865.

Two weeks after Lincoln's assassination, as the Civil War was coming to an end, Frederick Douglass wrote to his friend Senator Sumner to ask for help finding a clerkship for his son Lewis in the newly-formed Freedmen's Bureau. In a postscript, Douglass added, "The friends of freedom, all over the country have looked to you, and confided in you, of all men in the U.S. Senate, during all this terrible war. They will look to you all the more now that peace dawns, and the final settlement of our national troubles is at hand. God grant you strength equal to your day and your duties, is my prayer and that of millions." Sumner spent the entirety of his career working towards racial equality; he and Douglass corresponded frequently.

The papers of Charles Sumner are just one of many Civil War and abolitionist collections at the library, including papers of Abraham Lincoln, Thomas Wentworth Higginson, Wendell Phillips, William Lloyd Garrison, Frank Vizetelly, and others.

MS Am 1 (1902).
9¾ by 7¾ in.
Chiefly the gift of Edward L. Pierce, 1874, with later additions from the Pierce family in 1918 and 1942.

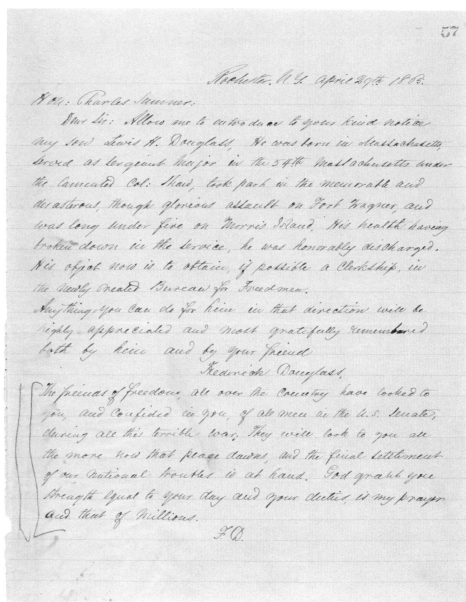

MARIANNE DWIGHT (1816–1901). *LOBELIA CARDINALIS,* (CARDINAL FLOWER), 1846.

In 1841, a group of Unitarians and Transcendentalists formed the utopian community Brook Farm in West Roxbury, Massachusetts. Among the group's founding members was novelist Nathaniel Hawthorne, who later fictionalized the experience in *The Blithedale romance* (1852). Marianne Dwight moved to the community in 1844 with her family. While living at Brook Farm, Dwight supported herself by painting fans and lampshades, as well as teaching art and Latin. On October 5, 1845, she wrote to her friend Anna Q. T. Parsons, "I now have a plan . . . of making some little books for sale . . . They are to be picture books—wild flowers, birds. . . .I intend to have the cover of colored Bristol-board, prettily stamped, like our fans and shades" (Amy L. Reed, ed., *Letters from Brook Farm*, Poughkeepsie, N. Y.: Vassar College, 1928, p. 120). This album of wildflowers seems to be one of those books, with a similar cover, and vibrant watercolors of the flowers Dwight loved.

MS Am 2625.
15 by 12½ in.
Edward and Bertha C. Rose acquisitions fund, the Stanley Marcus endowment for rare books, and the Amy Lowell fund, 2008.

AUBREY BEARDSLEY (1872–1898). SKETCH BOOK, 1891.

Despite an abbreviated life, Aubrey Beardsley is remembered for his distinctive black and white drawings from *The yellow book*, Oscar Wilde's *Salome* (1894), Pope's *The rape of the lock* (1896), and other works. This sketchbook, compiled by Beardsley when he was 19, contains forty-three drawings in pen and pencil.

While the collection of 1907 graduate Harry Elkins Widener (1885–1912) is housed in the Widener Memorial Room in Widener Library, it has been administered since 1969 through the Houghton Library reading room. A curator from among the Houghton staff retrieves collections, assists researchers, and gives tours of the room. Widener's collection of approximately 3,300 books, manuscripts, and drawings includes works by Charles Dickens, William Makepeace Thackeray, Kate Greenaway, George Cruikshank, and others.

HEW 1.3.4.
4½ by 10½ in. (when open).
Harry Elkins Widener Collection, 1915.

John Tenniel (1820–1914).
Study for "Alice's evidence,"
ca. 1864.

John Tenniel was already a prolific
and successful artist when Lewis
Carroll approached him to illustrate
Alice's adventures in Wonderland. Their
collaboration was a frustrating one:
Carroll closely supervised Tenniel,
visiting his studio frequently and
providing detailed suggestions for
the size and placement of each
illustration. Despite the tension
between the two men, it has become
impossible to think of Carroll's story
apart from Tenniel's artwork. His
illustrations are perhaps even more
recognizable than Carroll's own text,
and subsequent illustrators of the
book found it difficult to reinvent
Carroll's scenes and characters.

Houghton Library's collection of
Lewis Carroll, compiled primarily by
collector Harcourt Amory (Harvard
Class of 1876), includes numerous
editions of Carroll's works, including
the rare first edition of *Alice* presented
to Alice Liddell, the inspiration for
Carroll's character.

MS Eng 718.6 (12).
Graphite, heightened with ink and
Chinese white on paper. 6½ by 5 in.
Gift of Gertrude Chase Amory, 1927.

CHARLES SANDERS PEIRCE (1839–1914). GAME FRAGMENT, UNDATED.

The 150 boxes of papers of mathematician, chemist, philosopher, logician, and Cambridge, Massachusetts native, Charles Sanders Peirce (Harvard Class of 1859) reflect the incredible variety of subjects with which Peirce was conversant. This undated drawing of a labyrinthian maze, from a section of Peirce's papers on chess, cards, puzzles, and other games, illustrates a Peircean idea of the chaotic play of our paths through the world.

MS Am 1632 (1537).
17½ by 14 in.
Gift of Juliette Peirce, 1914–1915.

"G. W. James hard at work (reading)" _(caption within image)_

WILLIAM JAMES IN PURSUIT OF A CAREER

Before William James (1842–1910) became a respected Harvard professor and founded the field of modern psychology, he was a privileged young New Yorker looking for direction. Sketches of siblings Garth Wilkinson and Alice reveal his talent as an artist, but he was unsure if he had the requisite skill to be successful in that field. The lack of approval from his parents for such a career encouraged James to enroll at Harvard Medical School instead. Unenthusiastic about that endeavor, James joined an expedition to Brazil led by Harvard naturalist Louis Agassiz in 1865. Bouts of illness, including smallpox, turned James away from that career as well.

"G. W. James hard at work (reading),"
ca. 1863–1864.
MS Am 1092.2 (48).
Pencil. 4½ by 8½ in.
Gift of Henry James III, 1942.

H -

The lovercess of W. J

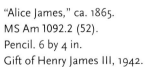

Drawing of Alice James?
H.J.

"Alice James," ca. 1865.
MS Am 1092.2 (52).
Pencil. 6 by 4 in.
Gift of Henry James III, 1942.

William James in Brazil
after an attack of smallpox,
1865.
MS Am 1092 (1185) #8.
3½ by 2 in.
Gift of the James family,
undated.

THE PICTORIAL AUTOBIOGRAPHY OF HALF MOON, AN UNCPAPA SIOUX CHIEF, BETWEEN 1868–1876.

MS Am 2337. 7¾ by 12 in. (when open).
Gift of Harriet J. Bradbury, 1930.

Found in a funerary tipi on the Little Bighorn battlefield in 1876, this ledger book containing seventy-seven drawings by Lakota Sioux and Cheyenne warriors depicts a series of conflicts known as "Red Cloud's War" from 1866–1868, as well as hunting and courting stories. Ledger books like this one were frequently taken by American Indian warriors from U.S. soldiers and filled with records of battles and other activities.

Extensive research by scholars at Harvard's Peabody Museum of Archaeology and Ethnology and members of the Standing Rock Sioux Tribe identified the artwork of at least six different warriors, who used indigenous and euroamerican materials to create the drawings, sometimes collaboratively.

THE AMERICAN BOARD OF COMMISSIONERS FOR FOREIGN MISSIONS ARCHIVE

One of the largest and most heavily used collections at Houghton Library, the ABCFM archive documents the lives of American missionaries and the people they met abroad from the early 19th century to the 1960s. Deposited at Houghton by the oldest organized missionary society in the United States, and spanning nearly a quarter-mile of shelving, the collection is used for multidisciplinary research on an almost daily basis.

Along with voluminous written accounts by missionaries are extensive collections of photographs. Pictured opposite are medical graduates with Dr. Kate Woodhull, a physician who worked and taught in a hospital in Fuzhou, China, from 1884–1912.

The collection also includes work produced by the communities among which the missionaries lived, such as this 1834 manuscript documenting the creation of a syllabic writing system for the Vai language, spoken in present-day Liberia and Sierra Leone. A note on the verso of the syllabary states, "It is but two years since it was first invented. The history of its invention is this. Some youngsters seeing the Americans exchanging letters, determined to have a system of writing in which they might communicate with each other in their own language . . . Some of the characters are Arabic, most of them are more fanciful. The characters stand for syllables, & not words."

"New invented native alphabet of Western Africa."
MS Vai 1.
10 by 8 in.
Deposited by the American Board of Commissioners for Foreign Missions, 1947.

74

Dr. Kate Woodhull and her medical graduates,
Fuzhou, China, ca. 1895 .
ABC 78.1, Box 49.
5½ by 7½ in.
Deposited by Wider Church Ministries, 1947.

EDWARD GORDON CRAIG (1872–1966), OWNER. ANNOTATED COPY OF *MACBETH*, 1892.

Heavily marked and interleaved, this copy of *Macbeth* was annotated over sixty-five years by Craig, an actor, director, and scenic designer. Each of his revisions is scrupulously dated, offering a chronology of his evolving interpretation. In the scene shown here, he exaggerates the witches' cavern into a volcanic crater around which sixty witches labor. Characteristic of his experiments with light and color, a shaft of limelight shines upward through the smoke billowing from beneath the stage. In 1934, he abandoned this idea altogether, preferring instead to "play the whole scene not to the 'scale of dragon' but to the scale of the 'eye of newt.'"

MS Thr 345 (15).
9 by 13 in. (when open).
Gift of Barry Bingham, Sr.; Edwin Binney III; Anna E. Crouse; Iris M. Fanger; Gannett Newspaper Foundation; Magowan Family Fund, Inc.; Emily L. McGregor; Jean Richmond; Arnold Rood; Waldo E. Stuart; and Helen D. Willard, 1979.

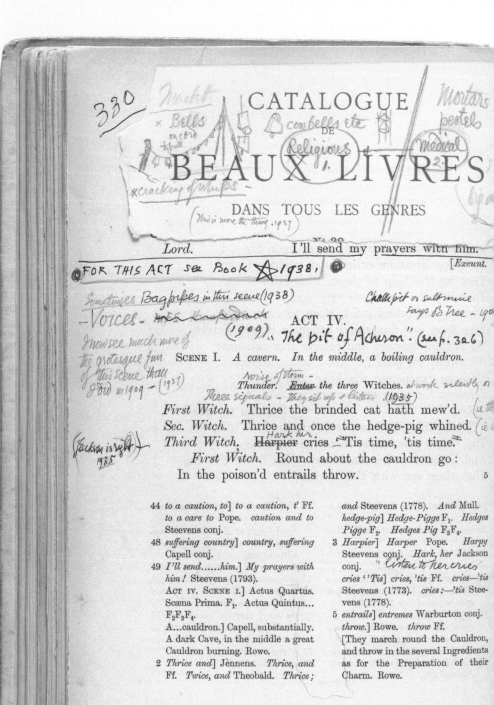

Volcano crater - & steam all around

Paint it in 6 or 7 different reds - Macbeth Black. 1904

a deep & big bell.

like a crater of a
- stuff boiling over like lava
ted & seen

I cancel all this page & the whole of this idea - EGC. 1934.

This scene is An amazing fine piece of theatre work   Let it be really Fantastic & theatrical.

3 witches out among the rocks & like rocks -
...ing out this & that which
...assistants sieze & carry it
...cauldron -

Three statues - Lemi { natural rock Sculpture }   no 1936

For rocks see mantegna - other prints -

The steam & smoke escape through the cracks in the masonry.

stage edge
orchestra

Macbeth CG.

Or the ruins of a Roman Theatre - in the midst of which the witches have assembled. (1909) Hmm!

EDWARD CURTIS (1868–1952). HOLLOW HORN BEAR AND OGALALA WOMAN FROM *THE NORTH AMERICAN INDIAN*, 1908.

Published between 1907 and 1930, American photographer and ethnographer Edward Curtis's haunting photographs of American Indians were captured as their traditional ways of life were rapidly disappearing. Called "Shadow Catcher" by his subjects, Curtis took over 40,000 photographs of members of over 80 tribes, also recording over 10,000 wax cylinders of languages and music.

Houghton's copy of the work was a gift to Harvard by J. P. Morgan, who helped Curtis finance the project.

US 10243.25.
Volume 3, *The Teton Sioux.*
The Yanktonai. The Assiniboin
([Seattle]: E. S. Curtis; [Cambridge, Mass.: The University Press],
1908). Brown-ink photogravures.
18 by 13½ in.
Gift of John Pierpont Morgan,
1918.

Hollow Horn Bear, plate 82.

Ogalala woman, plate 94.

THEODORE ROOSEVELT IN AFRICA, 1909–1910.

Following his second term as president, Theodore Roosevelt (1858–1919, Harvard Class of 1880) embarked on safari through what was then British East Africa. Always a voracious reader, TR brought fifty-nine titles bound in pigskin and packed, as he described in *African game trails*, "in a light aluminum and oil-cloth case, which, with its contents, weighed a little less than sixty pounds, making a load for one porter." The pigskin binding protected the books from the environment and heavy use: ". . . the books were stained with blood, sweat, gun oil, dust, and ashes; ordinary bindings would either have vanished or become loathsome," TR later wrote in *The outlook*. Fifty-five titles, and their original case, are now in the Theodore Roosevelt Collection at Houghton.

Pigskin Library and case, 13½ by 28 by 6 in. Bequest of Sarah Alden Derby Gannett, 2002.

TR reading in camp at Kijabe, Kenya, June, 1909. Roosevelt 560.61-164.
4½ by 3½ in. Gift, Theodore Roosevelt Association, 1943.

ALEXANDRE BENOIS (1870–1960).
SET DESIGN FOR ACT II OF *LE PAVILLON D'ARMIDE*,
1909.

The Howard D. Rothschild Collection on Ballets Russes includes manuscripts, letters, contracts, original set and costume designs for productions, objects, and photographs of Serge Diaghilev's famous ballet company. The collection was amassed by an American artist, and industrial engineer by training, Howard D. Rothschild, by purchase and by gifts of the Ballets Russes dancers and artists with whom he developed friendships.

Established in 1909 to promote Russian ballet and art in the West, the Ballets Russes gave rise a great number of outstanding dancers, choreographers, composers, and artists who recreated the art of ballet for the twentieth century, both in Europe and in the United States. *Le pavillon d'Armide* was conceived of and designed by Alexandre Benois, a Russian artist and one of the principal designers for the Ballets Russes, to the score of Nikolai Tcherepnin, and choreographed by Michel Fokine.

Nikolai Sergeev (1876–1951). Dance notation for *The sleeping beauty*, 1939.

One of the most famous ballets in the 19th-century classical repertory, *The sleeping beauty,* choreographed by Marius Petipa to the music of Peter Tchaikovsky, was first performed at the Imperial Mariinsky Ballet in 1890. This undated notation was created more than ten years after the premiere. It was first used by Sergeev for the staging of the famous 1921 Ballets Russes production at the Alhambra Theatre in London; and more recently by choreographer Aleksei Ratmansky for the American Ballet Theatre production in 2015.

MS Thr 245 (204).
14 by 8½ in.
F. E. Chase fund and Duplicate fund, 1969.

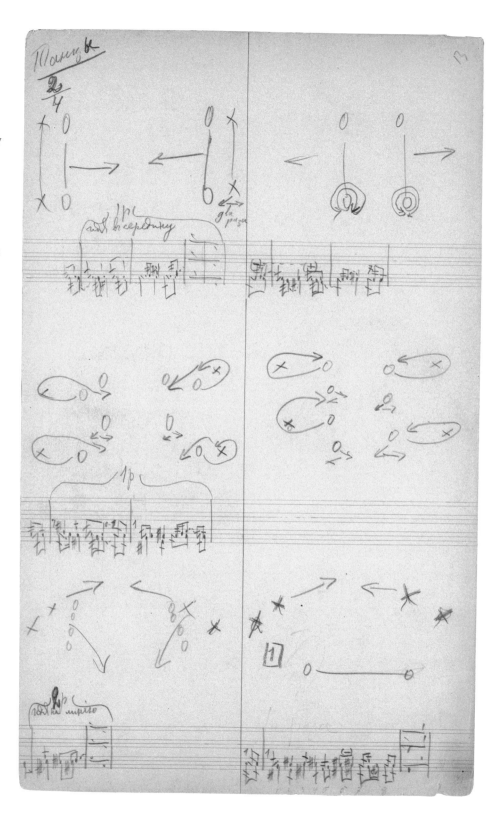

LYONEL FEININGER (1871–1956). PHOTOGRAPHS.

Already a highly-respected Expressionist painter, Bauhaus master Lyonel Feininger acquired a Voigtländer Bergheil camera in 1928 and found that the new medium inspired and enhanced his artwork. Houghton's collection of Feininger's work includes over 500 of his photographs, along with drawings and papers.

MS Ger 146.4 (291).
Effect of streetlights on a foggy night. Dessau; [1929–1931].
7 by 9½ in.
Gift of T. Lux Feininger, 1987.

MS Ger 146.4 (358).
Streetscene [sic], *double exposure.* [n.p.];
1929–1930.
7 x 9 in.
Gift of T. Lux Feininger, 1987.

VIRGINIA WOOLF (1882–1941). MONK'S HOUSE PHOTOGRAPH ALBUMS, 1863–1967.

The six Monk's House photograph albums contain over one thousand snapshots taken by Virginia Woolf, her sister Vanessa Bell, and other family members and friends, and candidly capture Woolf and friends at home and abroad.

AT RIGHT:
Cover of album 3, MS Thr 560.

OPPOSITE PAGE:
Gelatin silver prints, 4 by 3 in.

Gift of Frederick R. Koch, 1983.

MS Thr 560 (5). Virginia Woolf sitting in an armchair indoors, Monk's House, Rodmell, England. August 1, 1931.

MS Thr 560 (54). Leonard Woolf, Virginia Woolf, Roger Eliot Fry, and Margery Fry standing in front of the Olympieion, Athens, Greece. May 8, 1932.

MS Thr 560 (60). Virginia Woolf sitting on the beach, Aigina, Greece. May 6, 1932.

Allen Ginsberg (1926–1997), owner.
T. S. Eliot's *Collected poems, 1909–1935.*

Before he was a celebrated poet at the center of the Beat movement, Allen Ginsberg worked as a market researcher in New York, where in 1950 he bought a used copy of T. S. Eliot's poems. The pages of *The waste land* are covered in Ginsberg's marginalia, revealing a young writer, five years away from publishing *Howl,* attempting to work through Eliot's masterpiece.

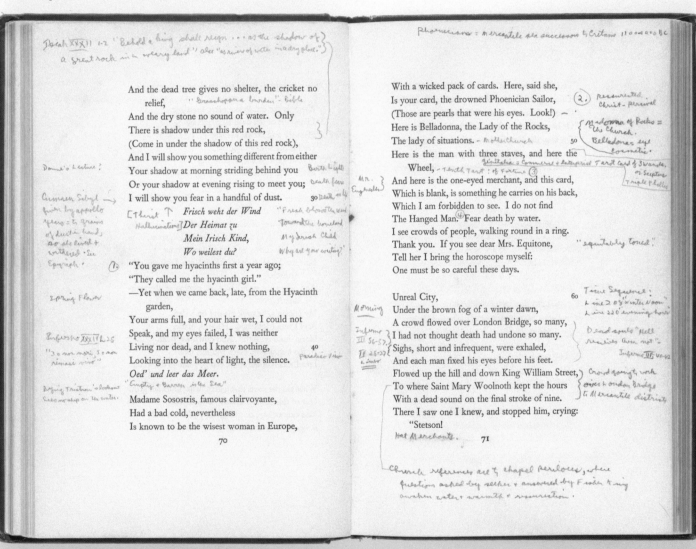

AC95.G4351.Zz936e.
8½ by 12 in. (when open).
Amy Lowell fund, 2008.

JOSÉ MARÍA CASTAÑÉ COLLECTION

Spanish entrepreneur José María Castañé's recent gift to the library includes over 15,000 papers, photographs, and books that document pivotal political and military events of the twentieth century. Among the many treasures in the collection are an image by Soviet Jewish realist photographer Mark Markov-Grinberg (1907–2003) of Red Army soldiers hiding in a trench to avoid detection during the Battle of Kursk, and artist Dame Laura Knight's rendering for the War Artists Advisory Committee of the processing of prisoners at the Nuremberg trials.

Gift of José María Castañé and the Fundación José María Castañé, 2015.

Mark Markov-Grinberg (1907–2003). *The Battle of Kursk and soldiers carrying out an attack*, 1943. 2014M-120 (8299). Gelatin silver print, 15 by 10 in.

Dame Laura Knight DBE, RA RSW (1877–1970). *Sketch Nuremberg Trials No. 10* prepared for the commissioned work "The Dock, Nuremberg," drawn during the processing of the prisoners, March 1946.

2014M-120 (1723). Charcoal on paper, 55½ by 43½ in.

THE WOODBERRY POETRY ROOM is a special collections reading room and audio archive located in Lamont Library and administered by Houghton Library. Founded in 1931, the Poetry Room features a circulating collection of 20th and 21st century English-language poetry, an encyclopedic array of literary magazines, a landmark collection of audio recordings (1933 to the present), and the Blue Star collection of rare books and chapbooks.

The centerpiece of the Poetry Room is its collection of over six thousand sound recordings on a range of media, including lacquer, shellac, and vinyl discs, magnetic tape (reel-to-reel and cassette), compact discs, and born-digital audio. The collection is, according to the late Nobel laureate Seamus Heaney, "indispensable: it contains not only the voices—from different times of their lives—of the greatest poets, but constitutes a living history of modern poetry." This vital tradition continues today with a dynamic range of public programs, as well as significant efforts to preserve, digitize, and provide access to its pivotal recordings for generations to come.

Sylvia Plath (1932–1963). Liner notes, in Plath's hand, on sound tape reel container. Recorded February 22, 1959, at the Fassett Recording Studio (Boston, Mass.) for the Woodberry Poetry Room. PS3566.L27 A6 1959x.

7 by 7 by 1 in.

Maurice Blanchot, novelist, literary theorist, philosopher, and journalist—though a reclusive figure in the literary world—had a profound impact on twentieth-century thinkers such as George Bataille, Jacques Derrida, and Gilles Deleuze, and others. Among Houghton's Blanchot holdings are page proofs of his 1969 major work, *L'entretien infini* (The infinite conversation). The proofs contain numerous handwritten annotations by Blanchot, along with typewritten sheets inserted into the proofs (of which some are small slips taped over pages and some are multiple pages in length).

The purchase of these proofs led to the acquisition six years later of Blanchot's archive, including working manuscripts, reading and research notes, notebooks, and substantial correspondence.

MS Fr 497.
9 by 8½ in.
Class of 1952 manuscript fund, the Amy Lowell fund, and the Patrick Grant second memorial fund (1928), 2009.

PAUL ROBESON (1898–1976) AS OTHELLO, 1943.

Paul Robeson, the son of an escaped slave, became one of his generation's most outspoken defenders of civil liberties. A graduate of Rutgers and Columbia Law School, he was a distinguished athlete, concert baritone, orator, and stage and screen actor. In 1929, racial intolerance in the U.S. forced Robeson to Britain, where he became the first black actor cast as Othello since Ira Aldridge a century earlier. Eminent director Margaret Webster paved the way for an American production in 1942, where a successful Broadway run culminated in a lengthy and culturally daring national tour. As a testament to Robeson's celebrity and bargaining clout, his contract for *Othello* denied to any segregated venue the pleasure of his enthralling performance.

MS Thr 612 (418).
78½ by 41 in.
Gift of Will Rapport, 1966.

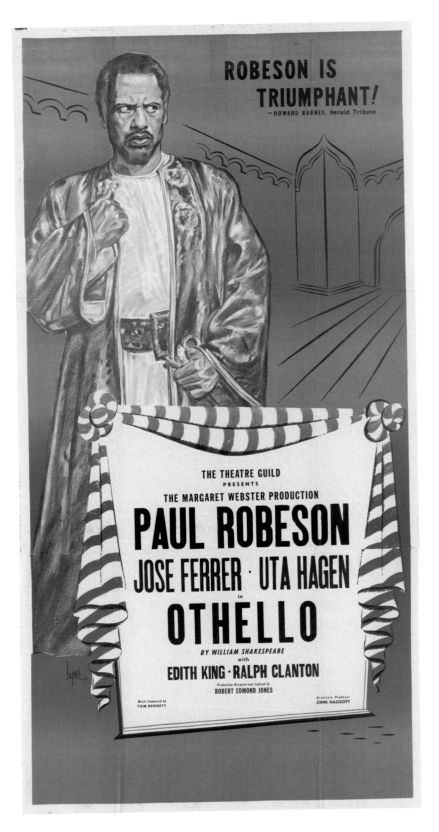

96

GORE VIDAL (1925–2012) AND TENNESSEE WILLIAMS (1911–1983).

In the spring of 1948, after the publication of his controversial third novel, *The city and the pillar,* Gore Vidal traveled to Europe, where he met playwright Tennessee Williams, fresh from the success of *A streetcar named Desire.* Vidal felt that "Tennessee was the greatest company on earth. . . . He had a wild sense of humor, grotesque, much like mine, and we just spent a lot of time parodying the world, mocking and burlesquing everything and everybody" (Fred Kaplan, *Gore Vidal: a biography;* New York: Doubleday, 1999, p. 265).

Houghton holds Vidal's papers and library, along with significant collections of Williams's manuscripts and playscripts.

Tennessee Williams to Gore Vidal, undated (late 1940s).
MS Am 2350 (2226).
11½ by 8½ in.

Williams and Vidal in Rome.
MS Am 2350 (4360).
3½ by 5 in.
Gift of Gore Vidal, 2001–2003.

Bright eyes!

This is glorious news about the play! Glorious plays are not usually written in such a short time, but Saroyan did it so why not you. I imagine that you will read it over after a while and decide it is slightly less glorious than you originally supposed in the first flush of exultation. That is nearly always the unhappy case. However there is no reason why it should not be the beginning of a glorious play, any-how. And I am hoping it is and will be. By all means do send it to me. When a thing goes that quickly it is a good sign, for it means that the impulse was vital and the vision was clear. Don't be surprised if it takes you several months more to make it as good as you first thought it was.

Windham and Sandy Campbell have come to Italy. I met them in Florence and we came down to Rome together and they are now putting up at the Inglaterra and are simply wild abo_____ ___ of them think it is glorious. I hope it doesN't brea_____ _____ We are looking at apartments this after_____ set up housekeeping, the four o_____ and swishing his little tail a_____ istra! There has been a terr_____ ones. Flanner (Janet) and h_____ tion. Yesterday we all went_____ Berlin Anne Zero by the man_____ arrived Janet said, "The ladies will si_____ gentleman in the rear." And Esther, the biggest w_____ looks like Wallace Beery in drag, said, "Ah-ha! Sex discrimina_____ They are a jolly bunch and the social life is considerably better than when there was just us girls, sunning ourselves like a bunch of lizards on the walk in front of Doney's. No word from Fritz and Russell who went off together. The French actor is still around but I haven't seen him. Poor La Traube! He has the clap now, the only one of us to be stricken, just when he was getting over the crab_____

Robert Lowell (1917–1977) and Elizabeth Bishop (1911–1979).

Poets Lowell and Bishop met in 1947, both at the beginning of their careers. They took to one another instantly; for Bishop it "was the first time I had ever actually talked with someone about how one writes poetry;" it was "like exchanging recipes for making a cake." (*Words in air;* New York: Farrar, Straus and Giroux, 2008, p. 810). Sometimes continents apart, Lowell and Bishop exchanged letters, poetry drafts, and books for thirty years. Each composed a number of poems about the other, including Lowell's poem "The Two Weeks' Vacation," of which this is an early draft; Bishop sent her heartbreaking elegy "North Haven" to friend Frank Bidart for comments in 1978.

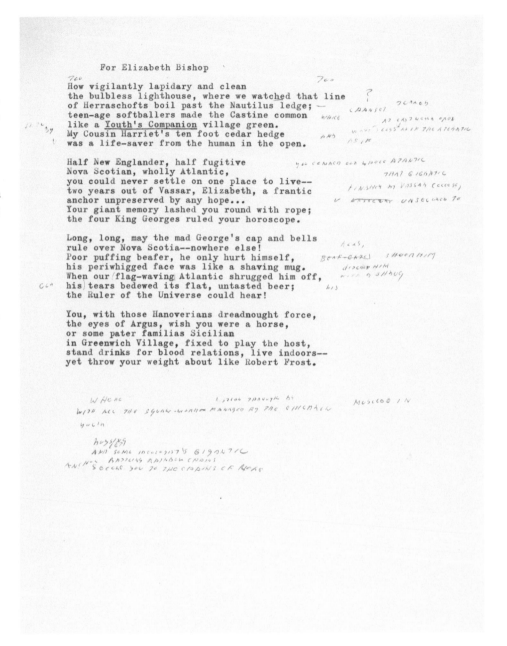

Robert Lowell, *For Elizabeth Bishop; flying to Rio de Janeiro 1956,* undated.
MS Am 1905 (2238).
11 by 8½ in.
Amy Lowell fund, 1973.

NORTH HAVEN
(In memoriam: R.T.S.L.)

I can make out the rigging of a schooner
a mile off; I can count
the new cones on the spruce. It is so still
the pale bay wears a milky skin, the sky
no clouds, except for one long, carded, horse's-tail.

(no feet / no feet) — ◄ The islands haven't shifted since last summer,
even if I like to pretend they have
- drifting, in a dreamy sort of way,
a little north, a little south or sidewise,
and that they're free within the blue frontiers of bay.   the - their ?

This month, our favorite one is full of flowers:
Buttercups, Red Clover, Purple Vetch,
Hawkweed still burning, Daisies pied, Eyebright,
the Fragrant Bedstraw's incandescent stars,
and more, returned, to paint the meadows with delight.

The Goldfinches are back, or others like them,
and the White-throated Sparrow's five-note song,
pleading and pleading, brings tears to the eyes.
Nature repeats herself, or almost does:
repeat, repeat, repeat; revise, revise, revise.

Years ago, you told me it was here
(in 1932?) you first "discovered girls"
and learned to sail, and learned to kiss.
You had "such fun", you said, that classic summer.
("Fun" - it always seemed to leave you at a loss...)

You left North Haven, anchored in its rock,
afloat in mystic blue... And now - you've left
for good. You can't derange, or re-arrange,
your poems again. (But the Sparrows can their songs.)
The words won't change again. Sad friend, you cannot change.

Dear Frank: there may be too much punctuation in this - possibly your
bad influence! But I wanted to have the sense just right my way, for
once - which is possibly just what you feel all the time... The flowers
are sort of like that Russian's wreath - the bird-songs, music, etc. -
but I hope this isn't too obvious. I think it's all right now, but who knows - ?

Thank you for your interest & help - much love - E.

Monday night -

Elizabeth Bishop, *North Haven*, 1978.
MS Am 2036 (1).
11 by 8½ in.
Amy Lowell fund, 1988.

ANGUS MCBEAN (1904–1990).
PORTRAITS.

Photographer Angus McBean captured the stars of the golden
age of British theater from the 1930s through the 1960s,
with a particular focus on productions of Shakespeare's plays.
Houghton's collection of McBean's work includes over 30,000
glass plate negatives, and is one of the most heavily used
resources in the Harvard Theatre Collection.

MS Thr 581.
All 6½ by 5 in.
Purchased from Angus McBean, 1970.

Laurence Olivier, undated.

Richard Burton as Hal in *Henry IV, Part II*, 1951.

Elizabeth Taylor in *Dr. Faustus*, 1966.

Moira Shearer, undated.

Marlene Dietrich, undated.

Audrey Hepburn, undated.

Vivien Leigh as Cleopatra in *Caesar and Cleopatra*, 1951.

Victoria Ocampo (1890–1979). Letter to Virginia Woolf, 1934.

Argentinian author, editor, and activist Victoria Ocampo founded the literary magazine and publishing house *Sur* in 1931, which would launch the careers of many of the most well-known writers of twentieth-century Central and South America. Ocampo's substantial archive at Houghton contains correspondence as well as the compositions of many of those writers.

Ocampo first encountered Virginia Woolf's work while living with Sylvia Beach in Paris in 1929; in Woolf she found a kindred spirit, another woman working in a field dominated by men. The two women met in London in 1934, and afterwards exchanged a series of deeply emotional letters. In this powerful letter to Woolf, Ocampo muses, "I do not like to eat and not feel fed. Under this aspect, I am ravenous. And I'm not ashamed to be hungry. Don't you think that love is our hunger for love? . . . Our hunger is very important. Things only exist for us when we are hungry and because of them." She later writes, "if there is anyone in the world who can give me courage and hope, it is you."

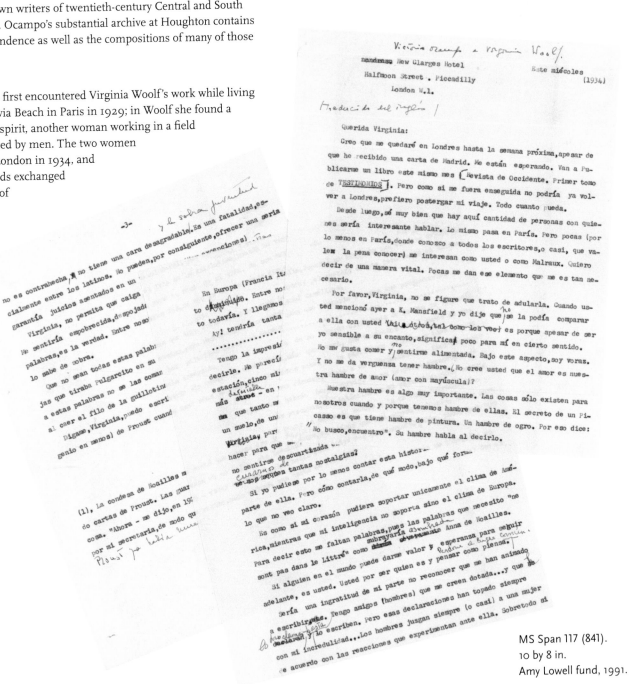

MS Span 117 (841).
10 by 8 in.
Amy Lowell fund, 1991.

John Updike's self-portraits, 1949.

The collection of novelist and critic John Updike (1932–2009, Harvard Class of 1954) comprises hundreds of volumes from Updike's library and over 350 boxes of papers, deposited box by box by Updike himself beginning in the 1960s. Among the papers is a collection of Updike's juvenilia, including material from his time as associate editor of the Shillington, PA, High School *Chatterbox*. Updike drew this cartoon of self-portraits for the first issue of his senior year.

MS Am 1793 (1).
Graphite, ink, and red typewriter ribbon on paper, 11 by 8½ in.
Gift of John Updike and purchase from the John Updike estate on the Amy Lowell fund, Charles Warren American History fund, and with gifts from generous donors, 2009.

Anne Eisner (1913–1995). Beauty salon, 1956.

Artist and ethnographer Anne Eisner and her husband Patrick Putnam, an anthropologist, ran a hotel, research camp, and medical clinic in what is now the Democratic Republic of the Congo, near the home of the Mbuti Pygmies, whom they studied. Eisner lived in the Congo on and off from 1946–1958, during a frequently violent period in the region. Eisner immersed herself in Congolese culture, and her paintings valorize the everyday lives of the people who surrounded her.

MS Am 2369 (65b).
Gouache on newsprint mounted on cardboard, 21 by 15 in.
Gift of Christie McDonald, 2006.

Wole Soyinka (1934–).
Prison diary, ca. 1967–1969.

"Books and all forms of writing have always been objects of
terror to those who seek to suppress truth," Nigerian playwright
and poet Wole Soyinka wrote in the preface to the published
edition of his diaries (1972). The first African to win a Nobel
Prize in Literature, Soyinka was imprisoned from 1967–1969 for
political activities. While in solitary confinement, Soyinka kept
diaries in the margins and between lines of text in the books he
was able to acquire, as well as on toilet paper and cigarette packs,
using ink he made himself. The diaries were smuggled out piece
by piece, reassuring Soyinka's readers that he was alive.

The Soyinka papers at Houghton contain five volumes of the
prison diary, in addition to numerous drafts of Soyinka's work,
correspondence, and other papers.

MS Thr 427 (19), vol. 1.
[Prison diary] Jerry Blunt, *The composite art of acting*.
(New York: Macmillan, 1966). 9 by 13½ in. (when open).
Amy Lowell fund, Harvard Theatre Collection funds, and funds
from the W. E. B. Du Bois Institute and the
President's Office, 1995.

Atelier Populaire posters, May 1968.

The civil unrest that erupted in Paris in 1968 generated a corresponding artistic movement, captured in hundreds of silkscreened posters created by students and hung throughout the city. Designed and printed by anonymous artists, the posters reproduced popular slogans of the movement and encapsulated the frustration and anger felt by the *soixante-huitards*.

A large collection of May 1968 posters came to Houghton as part of the monumental Julio Mario Santo Domingo Collection, encompassing over 50,000 items relating to drugs and drug use, 20th-century social protest movements, and popular culture. The 143 posters in the collection express the power of protest and the voice of students and workers fighting a right-wing government and the media the government controlled. The posters join other revolutionary and political movement archives at Houghton, including collections of the Black Panther, Solidarity, and Occupy Harvard movements, among others.

(52). *Je participe . . .* : silkscreened poster, 1968. 22½ by 17½ in.

FB9.A100.968p. Deposit, Julio Santo Domingo III, 2012.

(144). *La lutte continue*: postcard, 1968. 6 by 4 in.

(93). *La police vous parle tous les soirs à 20h*:
silkscreened poster, 1968.
13½ by 11½ in.

(135). [Hitler with a mask of de Gaulle]:
silkscreened poster, 1968.
10½ by 8 in.

(138). [Police with shield and baton]:
silkscreened poster with
spray-painted graffiti, 1968.
26 by 17 in.

AL HIRSCHFELD (1903–2003).
IRVING BERLIN, 1988.

American artist Al Hirschfeld is
best known for his black and white
caricatures of entertainers, since
his work, especially in the first
decades of his career, was intended
for the monochromatic medium
of newsprint. But he often worked
in color for theatrical posters and
magazines, like *Stereo review*, for
which he did full-page illustrations of
the recipient of the prestigious Mabel
Mercer Award.

The Harvard Theatre Collection holds
a significant collection of Hirschfeld
art and ephemera. Amassed over
many years by collector Mel Seiden
(Harvard Class of 1952, LL.B. 1955),
it includes hundreds of portraits,
production scenes, book illustrations,
political cartoons, and sketchbooks
Hirschfeld carried to theaters.

Melvin R. Seiden Collection.
Gouache on board, 16½ by 13 in.
Gift of Melvin R. Seiden, 1994.

ROBERT FLETCHER (1922–).
STAR TREK DRAWINGS, CA. 1979.

Bob Fletcher (Harvard Class of 1945) is best known as the costume designer for the first four *Star Trek* films. The first film's director, Robert Wise, tasked Fletcher with overhauling the garish wardrobe of the original series, when color broadcasts were a novelty. Wise wanted the film to look more "science fact" than "science fiction;" Fletcher answered with streamlined costumes in muted hues—and more of them—to add variety when a set change on the *Enterprise* was not possible. Fletcher also made over the alien Klingons at creator Gene Roddenberry's urging, giving them their distinctive ridged foreheads and feudal armor.

These sketches of a Klingon and William Shatner as Captain Kirk are not the only *Star Trek* items at Houghton; collections also include a guide for episode writers on the series' first season, film stills, screenplays, and novelizations.

2004MT-81.
Gift of Robert Fletcher, 2004.

Klingon.
Pencil and watercolor.
18½ by 13 in.

Captain Kirk.
Pencil and watercolor.
17½ by 12 in.

Black hero comics, 1972–2016.

Long celebrated by fans and collectors as substantive and important works of art, comic books and graphic novels have only recently begun to be studied by scholars. Among the significant collections of comic books, graphic novels, and fanzines at Houghton is a collection of comics featuring black heroes, from the first issue of *Luke Cage: hero for hire* in 1972 to the 2016 series of *Black Panther* authored by award-winning American writer Ta-Nehisi Coates.

AC95.A100.972b.
Black Panther #2, 1977; *The crew* #1, 2003; *Cage* #2, 1992; *By any means necessary: the life and times of Malcolm X,* 1993; *Luke Cage* #1, 1972; *Power Man & Iron Fist* #96, 1983; *Truth: red, white and black* #1, 2003.
All approx. 10 by 7 in.
Gift of Roger E. Stoddard, 2004.

PN6728.B523.C63.2016b.
Black Panther: a nation under our feet. Black Panther v. 6:1, Cover C variant by Sanford Greene.
10 by 7 in.
Roger Eliot Stoddard fund, 2016.

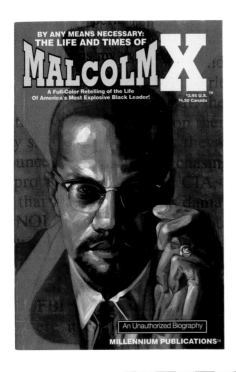

MacBook Air

Jamaica Kincaid (1949–). Laptop computers.

The papers of Antiguan-American writer and essayist Jamaica Kincaid are one of Houghton's most recent acquisitions. Twenty-first century writers create their work using very different media from their predecessors, and Houghton is committed to preserving that work, just as we carefully protect manuscripts on paper. Computer disks, drives, and other hardware are explored using a FRED (Forensic Recovery of Evidence Device)—a digital forensics machine that extracts files, drafts, and correspondence from outdated formats, allowing researchers to access them as easily as they do a cardboard box of files.

2015M-92.
Approx. 9 by 13 inches each.
Amy Lowell fund; Hutchins Center for African & African American Research; and the Bayard Livingston and Kate Gray Kilgour fund, 2016.

Acknowledgments

We are deeply indebted to the following
people for their assistance in compiling
this volume: President Drew Faust, Tom
Hyry, Dennis Marnon, Duncan Todd, Dale
Stinchcomb, Andrea Cawelti, Irina Klyagin,
Emilie Hardman, Leslie Morris, Mary Haegert,
Christina Davis, Mary Graham, Susan
Wyssen, the Houghton Library staff, David
Remington, Julia Featheringill, Bob Zinck,
and Mary Kocol. Publication of this volume
was made possible by a bequest from George
L. Lincoln '95, and by a fund established in
memory of William A. Jackson.

Image credits

Allen Ginsberg's copy of T. S. Eliot's *Collected poems*: copyright © Allen Ginsberg, used by permission of The Wylie Agency LLC.

Dame Laura Knight's *Sketch Nuremberg Trials No. 10* prepared for the commissioned work "The Dock, Nuremberg" 1946, © Reproduced with permission of The Estate of Dame Laura Knight DBE RA 2016. All rights reserved.

Maurice Blanchot, *L'entretien infini* page proofs, with permission of the Estate of Maurice Blanchot.

Tennessee Williams, letter to Gore Vidal, copyright © Tennessee Williams. Reprinted by permission of Georges Borchardt, Inc. for the Estate of Tennessee Williams.

John Updike's sketches for *Chatterbox* copyright © John H. Updike Literary Trust. Used by permission. All rights reserved.

Anne Eisner's painting "Beauty Salon" reproduced with permission of Christie McDonald.

Al Hirschfeld's portrait of Irving Berlin copyright © The Al Hirschfeld Foundation, www.AlHirschfeldFoundation.org.

Robert Fletcher's drawings for *Star Trek* reproduced with permission of Mr. Fletcher.

HOUGHTON LIBRARY AT 75: A Celebration of its Collections

was designed and typeset in FF Scala and FF Scala Sans by

Duncan G. Todd. The book was printed by Universal

Wilde, Inc., Westwood, Massachusetts, on Sappi McCoy

Silk 100 lb. text and 100 lb. cover, and Smyth sewn

by HF Group Acmebinding, Charlestown,

Massachusetts. One thousand copies

were bound in paper covers and two

hundred copies in Cialux midnight

blue cloth over boards.